Let Us Pray

Compiled by

Keith D. Walker

Copyright © 2024 Keith D. Walker
All Rights Reserved
Published by

Calgary, Saskatoon, Kingston, Wellington, NZ
ISBN: 978-1-304-8396-9

Boreal Chickadee cover photo by longstanding friend, Bryan Roset

Copies of this book may be ordered from: Lulu.ca, Lulu.com, Amazon.com or Amazon.ca

To worship is to quicken the conscience by the holiness of God, to feed the mind with the truth of God, to purge the imagination by the beauty of God, to open the heart to the love of God, to devote the will to the purpose of God.[1]

Loving Lord Jesus Christ, Son of God, *have mercy on me a sinner.* Help me to *continually mature* in my **trust** in You as I *experience* Your profound **goodness** and **justice** - and as my *conscience is quickened* by Your **holiness**, my *spirit is filled* with Your unquenchable **hope**, as my *mind is fed* by Your **truth**, as my *imagination is inspired* by Your **beauty**, as my *heart is compelled* by Your **love** and as my *will is engaged* with diligence in the call to fulfill Your magnificent **purposes**. I need You Lord Jesus. I love You Lord Jesus Christ. I give myself to You O Triune God, Father, Son, and Holy Spirit. Amen.

---

[1] William Temple. I came across this lovely description of worship, set forth in the order of service booklet in Salisbury Cathedral, Salisbury, UK. These five elements by William Temple have since helped frame my worship.

Acknowledgements for Let Us Pray Book

I am grateful to God for Viv, my beautiful wife and best friend for well over 40 years. Together we acknowledge, with gratefulness, the profound influence of our family on our lives. We love them and we've never been so dependent on God as we have been in our entrusting our children, now adults, to Him. James Houston, Eric Kenton, Graham MacKenzie, and Gillian Karyn are truly wonderful people to be with. We also celebrate the gifts of their marriage partners (Martha, SJ, Ali, and Cody) AND – our grandchildren. God is Good.

I also want to acknowledge our Circle Group of friends. We are extremely grateful for each member of this group with whom we meet with almost weekly. They are true friends who pray with and for us and our family; we are honoured to join them to pray and care for and about our families and the circumstances of life. We have known these fine people for 30-40+ years.

Both Viv and I are also thankful for the colleagues we work with in our roles with the Saskatchewan Health Authority, the University of Saskatchewan and the Mid-west District of the Alliance Canada.

Keith D. Walker
January 2024
Saskatoon

****

O God, with all my heart, I long for You. Come, transform me to be a Christ-centered, Spirit-empowered, mission-focused person, multiplying disciples everywhere.[2]

---

[2] Vision Prayer, Alliance Canada

Introduction to this Resource

We all have a deep longing that comes with being human. For my part, I desperately want the notice and attention of God. This is "designed into me," a longing and thirst for significance and identity. I want to hear Him, to be heard and to be present with Him. My identity and personhood derive from the Triune God who loves me, as He loves each of us.

Prayer makes a difference; it is efficacious means for connecting with God. Prayer is the space where I open up to my heavenly Father to walk with Him and talk with Him along life's way – for He cares deeply for me; He deeply care for each of us. I know he wants my attention, even more than I want His. He calls out to me, saying:

Say you love Me; tell Me that you love Me. Say that I am the One that you'll come running to; to hold you through the rain. Say you love Me and there is no one else above Me. Open up your heart to Me; I'll always be – all you'll ever need. Say you love Me.

The brilliant musical group - Naturally 7 wrote these vocal play lyrics and I think these beautifully capture the heart of God's desire to fellowship with me, and with you. This is His open invitation for me to find a place to BE with Him, as He is with me.

This book is a derivative and refreshed book from other prayer helps that I've assembled over the years for my own use. I do hope it might be useful to those with kindred spirit. It is a book of prayers that have helped my expressions of dependence on God and my ongoing renewal of devotion to Him.

As an apprentice of the Lord Jesus Christ, I reiterate that prayer is about communing with my Creator, Redeemer, Healer, Sanctifier, my Transforming Friend.

The **first** section of this book begins with several open pages for writing down names and items for prayer. *Feel free to write in this book (anywhere) – there are lots of spaces for you to do so.* The **second** short section has a focus on the attributes of God. After reminding oneself of who God is then prayer can be the safe place where we can be honest and where we can say "thy will be done, O LORD." This is a guide to worship and prayer using the attributes of God. The **third** section contains two traditional Christian creeds and a number of traditional prayers. I have also provided the Southwell Litany which I find helpful as I seek to walk humbly and worthily according to my calling and as I ask for cleansing from my sin and empowerment for leaning into Jesus and all He has for me. The **fourth** section is a fairly comprehensive list of prayer prompts to use to "pray around the world" for groups and concerns that we want to bring before the throne of God. The **fifth** and largest section of this devotional book is inspired by reading and praying with the Psalms. I've provided these scriptures from the Amplified Bible.[3] Ideally a person might read the Scripture passages, as I have done, and find the prayers to be a form of response to the heart cry of the Psalmist (Lectio Divina or "divine reading"). There are 62 prayers for two months or evening and morning prayers for one month. The small boxes make using the prayers in any order easy to track,

---

[3] The AMP was the first Bible project of The Lockman Foundation. Its goal was to take both word meaning and context into account to accurately translate the original text from one language into another. Multiple English word equivalents to each key Hebrew and Greek word clarify and amplify meanings that may otherwise have been concealed by the traditional translation method. The first edition was published in 1965. From https://www.biblegateway.com/versions/Amplified-Bible-AMP/

especially for periodic use or routine discipline. Of course, prayer is a platform for us to bring concerns, petitions, supplications, and to engage God's workings in my life and in the lives of others. These prayers might be prayed daily or occasionally. For the **sixth** section, I have merely gathered together the blessings or benedictions from Scripture and tradition. These can be personalized and offered through prayers for others by simply inserting the names of people or groups in the praying of the blessing. The **seventh** section provides a list of concerns, supplications and intercessions that may be used in prayer times. In the **eighth** section, there is an adaptation of a classic sermon on the person of the Lord Jesus Christ that I have used to worship Him and the **ninth, and final** section is a prayer that makes use of well over 200 names of God from Scripture. As I pray with this, I am remind of who God is; I worship Him in His worthiness.

Jesus said: therefore I tell you, do not be anxious about your life, what you will eat or what you will drink, or about your body, what you will put on. Is not life more than food and the body more than clothing?

Look at the birds of the air: They neither sow nor reap nor gather into barns, and yet your heavenly Father feeds them. Are you not of more value than they? Why, even the hairs of your head are numbered. Do not be afraid. And which of you by being anxious can add a single hour to his or her life?

For you did not receive the spirit of slavery to fall back into fear, but you received the Spirit of adoption as sons/daughters, by whom we cry Abba! Father![4]

---

[4] Matthew 6:25-34; Luke 12:7; Romans 8:15

Personalized Prayer Prompts and Lists[5]

[For written notes]

Immediate Family Members

Extended Family Members

Neighbours

Friends and Families of Friends

---

[5]Church House Publishings (UK) – *Time to Pray*, Baker Books – *Seeking God's Face*, and Faith Alive Christian Resources (USA) – *Prayers of the People* are three of numerous references that have helped me to develop the lists found in this prayer book.

Friends, Family, and Others with Special Needs

Co-workers, Colleagues, Fellow Students

Church Body and their Particular Needs

Particular Ministries

Particular Prayer Requests

Prayer with the Attributes of God[6]

Of course, worship involves awareness of God, awe in His presence, and adoration of Him. We are in awe because of the revelation of His inexhaustible excellences and acts of creation and redemption. Worship is our affirmation of His supreme and exclusive worthiness, through our humble praise of all He is and does.[7] Nehemiah and author of Hebrews said it this way: Stand up and bless the LORD your God forever and ever! Blessed be Your glorious Name, which is exalted above all blessing and praise! You alone are the LORD; You have made heaven, the heaven of heavens, with all their host, the earth and everything on it, the seas and all that is in them, and You preserve them all. The host of heaven worships You. Through Christ then, let us continually offer up a sacrifice of praise to God, that is, the fruit of the lips that give thanks to His Name.[8]

---

[6] These attributes of God are qualities that form the essence of God. There are other attributes (natural and moral) that could be indicated (this is not an exhaustive list). A god without any one of these attributes is not the God of the Bible

[7] Vernon Grounds and Leslie Flynn

[8] Nehemiah 9:5, 6 and Heb. 13:15

May I be ever mindful of Who it is that I bow before, as I pray: Creator and Redeemer, I worship You as the infinite,[9] omnipresent,[10] omnipotent,[11] omniscient,[12] wise,[13] providential,[14] immutable,[15] sovereign,[16] incomprehensible[17] God of the Bible. You are accessible,[18] simple,[19] one,[20] triune,[21] spirit,[22] self-existent[23] and self-sufficient,[24] immanent,[25] transcendent,[26] eternal,[27] and immense.[28] You are the jealous[29] God of wrath.[30] You are holy,[31] impeccable,[32] righteous,[33] just,[34] true,[35] faithful,[36] longsuffering,[37]

---

[9] 1 Kings 8:22–27; Jeremiah 23:24

[10] Psalms 139:7–12; Jeremiah 23:24; 1 Kings 8:27.

[11] Genesis 18:14; Revelations 19:6; Matthew 19:26

[12] Psalms 139:2–6; Isaiah 40:13–14; 66;1; Psalms 90:2; 102:12; 139:7-10; 145:3; 147:5; Hebrews 4:13; Romans 11:34; I Kings 8:27; Jeremiah 23:23, 24; Acts 17:27, 28; Job 11:7-10; 1 John 3:20; Romans 16:27; I Kings 8:29; Psalm 139:1-16; Isaiah 46:10; Ezekiel 11:5; Acts 15:18; John 21:17; Hebrews 4:13

[13] Proverbs 3:19; 1 Timothy 1:17; Romans 11:33; I Corinthians 2:7; Ephesians 1:6, 12, 14; Colossians 1:16

[14] Acts 17:25

[15] Hebrews 1:10–12; 13:8; James 1:17; Malachi 3:6; Hebrews 6:17; Numbers 23:19; Psalms 33:11; 102:27; James 1:17

[16] Isaiah 46:9–11; Genesis 50:20; Acts 2:23

[17] Job 11:7–19; Romans 11:33

[18] Deuteronomy 4:7. Psalm 27:4; Matthew 6:6; John 14:6; Ephesians 2:13; 3:12; Hebrews 4:16; 7:25; 10:22; James 4:8

[19] The simplicity of God means that God is a unified being – that He is one essence

[20] Mark 12:29; Ephesians 4:6; Deuteronomy 6:4–5; Isaiah 44:6–8

[21] 1 John 5:7; Matthew 28:19; 2 Corinthians 13:14

[22] John 4:24

[23] Exodus 3:13–14; Psalms 33:11; 115:3; Isaiah 40:18 ff.; Daniel 4:35; John 5:26; Romans 11:33-36; Acts 17:25; Revelations 4:11.

[24] Psalms 50:10–12; Acts 17:25; the aseity of God

[25] Acts 17:28

[26] Isaiah 57:15

[27] Deuteronomy 33:27; Psalm 90:2; Psalm 90:2; 1 Timothy 1:17

[28] Isaiah 40:28; 1 Kings 8:27

[29] Exodus 20:5-6

[30] Exodus 15:7; Deuteronomy 9:19; Psalm 69:24; John 3:36

[31] Leviticus 19:2; 1 Peter 1:15; Exodus 15:11; Isaiah 57:15; Isaiah 6:3; Revelation 4:8

[32] Hebrews 6:18

[33] Romans 1:17

[34] Psalms 119:137; 99:4; Isaiah 33:22; Romans 1:32

[35] John 17:3; Titus 1:1–2; Numbers 23:19; I Corinthians 1:9; II Timothy 2:13; Hebrews 10:23; Titus 1:2

[36] Deuteronomy 7:9; Psalms 89:1–2

[37] Romans 2:4; 9:22; I Peter 3:20; II Peter 3:16

good,[38] merciful,[39] gracious,[40] and loving.[41] All that You will do and have done and everything about You is worthy.[42] I worship You in the beauty of Your perfections.

---

[38] Psalms 107:8; 36:6; 104:21; 145:8, 9, 16; Matthew 5:45; Acts 14:17

[39] Psalms 103:8–17; Nehemiah 9:17b

[40] Psalms 111:4; 1 Peter 5:10; Ephesians 1:6, 7; 2:7-9; Titus 2:11; Exodus 34:5-6; 1 Peter 2:2, 3; God has compassion, is slow to anger and is pardoning.

[41] John 3:16; Romans 5:8; Luke 1:64, 72, 78; Romans 15:9; 9:16, 18; Ephesians 2:4; 1 John 4:16

[42] Romans 11:22; the omni-benevolence of God

Selected Creeds and Traditional Prayers

The Apostles' Creed

I believe in [You,] the Father almighty, maker of heaven and earth; and in Jesus Christ Your only Son my Lord; who was conceived by the Holy Spirit, born of the Virgin Mary, suffered under Pontius Pilate, was crucified, dead, and buried. He descended into hell. The third day He rose again from the dead. He ascended into heaven, and sits on Your right hand, Father almighty. From there He shall come to judge the quick and the dead. I believe in the Holy Ghost, the holy catholic Church, the communion of saints, the forgiveness of sins, the resurrection of the body, and the life everlasting. Amen.

The Nicene Creed

I believe in [You] one God, the Father almighty, maker of heaven and earth, of all things visible and invisible. I believe in [You] one Lord Jesus Christ, the Only Begotten Son of God, born of the Father before all ages. God from God, Light from Light, true God from true God, begotten, not made, consubstantial with the Father; through him all things were made. For us men and for our salvation he came down from heaven, and by the Holy Spirit was incarnate of the Virgin Mary, and became man. For our sake he was crucified under Pontius Pilate, he suffered death and was buried, and rose again on the third day in accordance with the Scriptures. He ascended into heaven and is seated at the right hand of the Father. He will come again in glory to judge the living and the dead and his kingdom will have no end. I believe in the Holy Spirit, the Lord, the giver of life, who proceeds from the Father and the Son, who with the Father and the Son is adored and glorified, who has spoken through the prophets. I believe in one, holy, catholic and apostolic Church. I confess one Baptism for the forgiveness of sins and I look forward to the resurrection of the dead and the life of the world to come. Amen.

The Southwell Litany[43]

From moral weakness, from hesitation, from fear of humankind and dread of responsibility; strengthen me with courage to speak the truth in love and self-control; and alike from the weakness of hasty violence and from weakness of judgment, cowardice: SAVE AND HELP ME, O LORD.

From the indecision that can make no choice and from the irresolution that carries no choice into action; strengthen my eye to see and my will to choose the right, the good and the virtuous; and from losing opportunities to serve You, and from perplexing myself and others with uncertainties: SAVE AND HELP ME, O LORD.

From infirmity of purpose, from want or earnest care and interest, from sluggish indolence and slack indifference, and from all spiritual deadness of heart: SAVE AND HELP ME, O LORD.

From dullness of conscience, from feeble sense of duty from thoughtless disregard of consequences to others, from a low idea of the obligations of my calling, and from half-heartedness in my service: SAVE AND HELP ME, O LORD.

From weariness in continuing struggles, from dependency in failure and disappointment, from overburdening sense of

---

[43] A litany is a series of petitions used in worship, usually with a recurring formula where leader makes a statement and the people respond. The *Southwell Litany* was written by George Ridding (March 16, 1828 - August 30, 1904). He was an English headmaster and 1st Bishop of Southwell, England. Originally entitled *A Litany of Remembrance*.

unworthiness, from morbid fancies of imaginary backsliding; raise me to a lively hope in mercy and in the power of faith; and from all exaggerated fears and vexations: SAVE AND HELP ME, O LORD.

From self-conceit, vanity, and boasting, from delight in supposed success and superiority; raise me to the modesty and humility of true sense and taste and reality; and from all the harms and hindrances of offensive manners and self-assertion: SAVE AND HELP ME, O LORD.

From affectation and untruth, conscious or unconscious, from pretense and hypocrisy, from impulsive self-adaptation to the moment to please persons or make circumstances easy; strengthen me to true simplicity; and from all false appearances: SAVE AND HELP ME, O LORD.

From love of flattery, from over-ready belief in praise, from dislike of criticism, and from the comfort of self-deception in persuading myself that others think better of me than I am: SAVE AND HELP ME, O LORD.

From all love of display and sacrifice to popularity, from thinking of myself and forgetting You in my worship: Hold my mind in spiritual reverence; and from self-glorification in all my words and works: SAVE AND HELP ME, O LORD.

From pride and self-will, from the desire to have my way in all things, from overweening love of my own ideas, and blindness to the value of others, from resentment against opposition and contempt for the claims of others: Enlarge the generosity of my heart and enlighten the fairness of my judgments; and from all selfish arbitrariness of temper: SAVE AND HELP ME, O LORD.

From jealousy, whether of equals or superiors, from grudging others' success, from impatience of submission and eagerness for authority: Give me the spirit of common fellowship to share loyally with fellow-workers in all true proportion; and from all insubordination to just law and proper authority: SAVE AND HELP ME, O LORD.

From all hasty utterances of impatience, from the retort of irritation and the taunt of sarcasm, from all infirmity of temper in provoking or being provoked; and from all idle words that may do hurt: SAVE AND HELP ME, O LORD.

In all times of temptation to follow pleasure, to leave duty for amusement, to indulge in distraction, dissipation, dishonesty, or debt, or to degrade my high calling and forget my solemn vows; and in all times of frailty in my flesh: SAVE AND HELP ME, O LORD.

In all times of ignorance and perplexity as to what is right and best to do; direct me with wisdom to judge aright, and order my ways, and overrule my circumstances by Your good Providence, and in all my mistakes and misunderstandings: SAVE AND HELP ME, O LORD.

From strife, partisanship, and division, from magnifying my certainties to condemn all differences, from building systems to exclude all challenges, and from all arrogance in my dealings with others: SAVE AND HELP ME, O LORD.

Give me a knowledge of myself: my power and weaknesses, my spirit, my sympathy, and imagination, my knowledge, my truth; teach me by the standard of Your Word, by the judgments of others, by examination of myself; give me an earnest desire to strengthen myself continually by study, diligence, prayer, and meditation; and from all fancies, delusions, and prejudices of habit, or temper, or society: SAVE AND HELP ME, O LORD.

Give me true knowledge of others, in their difference from me and in their likeness to me, that I may deal with their real selves measuring their feelings by my own, but patiently considering their varied lives and thoughts and circumstance; and in all my dealings with them, from false judgments of my own, from misplaced trust and distrust, from misplaced giving and refusing, from misplaced praise and blame: SAVE AND HELP ME, O LORD.

Chiefly I pray that I may know You and see You in all Your works, always feel Your presence near, hear You and know Your call: Let Your Spirit be my will, Your Word, my word; and in all my shortcomings and infirmities, may I have sure faith in Your mercy: SAVE AND HELP ME, O LORD.

Finally, I pray, blot out my past transgressions, heal the evils of my past negligences and ignorances, and help me to amend my past mistakes and misunderstandings; uplift my heart to new love, new energy, new devotion, that I may be unburdened from the grief and shame of past unfaithfulness; and go forth in Your strength to persevere, through success and failure.

"I Praise You" Prayer[44]

I praise You, O God; I acknowledge You to be the Lord. All the earth worships You, the Father everlasting. To You all angels cry aloud, the heavens and all the powers that reign. To You cherubim and seraphim continually do cry: Holy, holy, holy, Lord God of Sabbath; heaven and earth are full of the majesty of Your glory. The glorious company of the apostles praise You. The goodly fellowship of the prophets praise You. The noble army of martyrs praise You. The holy Church throughout all the world acknowledges You, the Father, of an infinite majesty, Your adorable, true, and only Son, also the Holy Spirit the Comforter.

You are the King of glory, O Christ. You are the everlasting Son of the Father. When You took upon Yourself to deliver humankind, You humbled Yourself to be born of a virgin. When You had overcome the sharpness of death, You opened the kingdom of heaven to all believers. You sit at the right hand of God, in the glory of the Father. I believe that You will come to be our judge. I therefore pray that You would help Your servant, whom You have redeemed with Your precious blood. Make me, and those I love, to be numbered with Your saints, in glory everlasting.

---

[44] *Te Deum laudamus*

Family Prayer

The Lord be with me and those I know and love. Our Father, who is in heaven, hallowed be Your name, Your kingdom come, Your will be done, on earth as it is in heaven. Give me this day my daily bread. And forgive me my trespasses, as I forgive those who have trespassed against me. And lead me not into temptation, but deliver me from evil. For Yours is the kingdom, and the power, and the glory, for ever and ever. Amen.

The Universal Prayer[45]

Lord, I believe in You: increase my faith. I trust in You: strengthen my trust. I love You: let me love You more and more. I am sorry for my sins: deepen my sorrow. I worship You as my first beginning, I long for You as my last end, I praise You as my constant helper, and call on You as my loving protector. Guide me by Your wisdom, correct me with Your justice, comfort me with Your mercy, protect me with Your power. I offer You, Lord, my thoughts: to be fixed on You, my words: to have You for their theme, my actions: to reflect my love for You, my sufferings: to be endured for Your greater glory. I want to do what You ask of me: In the way You ask, for as long as You ask, because You ask it.

Lord, enlighten my understanding, strengthen my will, purify my heart, and make me holy. Help me to repent of my past sins and to resist temptation in the future. Help me to rise above my human weaknesses and to grow stronger as a Christian. Let me love You, my Lord and my God, And see myself as I really am: A pilgrim in this world, a Christian called to respect and love all whose lives I touch, those under my authority, my friends and my enemies. Help me to conquer anger with gentleness, greed by

---

[45] Attributed to Pope Clement XI (1649 –1721)

generosity, apathy by fervour. Help me to forget myself and reach out toward others. Make me prudent in planning, courageous in taking risks. Make me patient in suffering, unassuming in prosperity. Keep me, Lord, attentive at prayer, temperate in food and drink, diligent in my work, firm in my good intentions.

Let my conscience be clear, my conduct be without fault, my speech blameless, and my life well-ordered. Put me on guard against my human weaknesses. Let me cherish Your love for me, keep Your law, and come at last to Your salvation. Teach me to realize that this world is passing, that my true future is the happiness of heaven; that life on earth is short, and the life to come eternal. Help me to prepare for death with a proper fear of judgment, but a greater trust in Your goodness. Lead me safely through death to the endless joy of heaven. Grant this through Christ my Lord. Amen.

Prayer of Saint Patrick[46]

I arise today through a mighty strength: the invocation of the Trinity, through a belief in the Three-ness, through confession of the Oneness of the Creator of creation. I arise today through the strength of Christ's birth and His baptism, through the strength of His crucifixion and His burial, through the strength of His resurrection and His ascension, through the strength of His descent for the judgment. I arise today through the strength of the love of cherubim, in obedience of angels, in service of archangels, in the hope of resurrection to meet with reward, in the prayers of patriarchs, in the preachings of the apostles, in the faith of confessors, in the innocence of virgins, in the deeds of righteous men and women. I arise today through the strength of heaven; light of the sun, splendor of fire, speed of lightning, swiftness of the wind, depth of the sea, stability of the earth, firmness of the

---

[46] Breast Plate Prayer "Lorica" ca. 377.

rock. I arise today through God's strength to pilot me; God's might to uphold me, God's wisdom to guide me, God's eye to look before me, God's ear to hear me, God's word to speak for me, God's hand to guard me, God's way to lie before me, God's shield to protect me, God's hosts to save me from snares of the devil, from temptations of vices, from every one who desires me ill, afar and near, alone or in a multitude.

I summon today all these powers between me and evil, against every cruel merciless power that opposes my body and soul, against incantations of false prophets, against black laws of pagandom, against false laws of heretics, against craft of idolatry, against spells of bad people and smiths and wizards, against every knowledge that corrupts a person's body and soul.

Christ shield me today against poison, against burning, against drowning, against wounding, so that reward may come to me in abundance. Christ with me, Christ before me, Christ behind me, Christ in me, Christ beneath me, Christ above me, Christ on my right, Christ on my left, Christ when I lie down, Christ when I sit down, Christ in the heart of every man who thinks of me, Christ in the mouth of every man who speaks of me, Christ in the eye that sees me, and Christ in the ear that hears me. I arise today through a mighty strength, the invocation of the Trinity, through a belief in the Three-ness, through a confession of the Oneness of the Creator of creation.

Prayer of Saint Francis of Assisi

Lord, make me an instrument of Your peace. Where there is hatred, let me sow love; where there is injury, pardon; where there is doubt, faith; where there is despair, hope; where there is darkness, light; where there is sadness, joy. O, Divine Master, grant that I may not so much seek to be consoled as to console; to be understood as to understand; to be loved as to love. For it is in giving that I receive; it is in pardoning that I am pardoned; it is in dying that I am born again to eternal life.

A Litany for Life

Lord, have mercy. Lord, have mercy. Christ, have mercy. You breathed life into Adam,[47] Lord, You give me life! You formed Eve[48] from flesh, Lord, You give me life! You heard the cry of innocent blood,[49] Lord, You give me life! You spared the life of Cain,[50] Lord, You give me life! You saved Noah[51] from the flood, Lord, You give me life! You filled Sarah's[52] barren womb, Lord, You give me life! You gave Abraham a son,[53] Lord, You give me life! You preserved the life of Jacob,[54] Lord, You give me life! You punished those who took life,[55] Lord, You give me life! You place before me life and death,[56] Lord, You give me life! You

---

[47] Genesis 2:7

[48] Genesis 9:5-6

[49] Genesis 4:16

[50] Genesis 8:16

[51] Genesis 21:2

[52] Genesis 21:3

[53] Genesis 32:31

[54] Numbers 35:31

[55] Deuteronomy 30:19

[56] Ruth 4:14

restore lost life,[57] Lord, You give me life. You nourish the aged and the weak,[58] Lord, You give me life! You delivered Saul from David,[59] Lord, You give me life! You redeemed the life of David,[60] Lord, You give me life! You gave Solomon length of days,[61] Lord, You give me life! You raised the child by Elijah's cry,[62] Lord, You give me life! You are the Life that is the light of all human beings,[63] Lord, You give me life! You are the Bread of Life,[64] Lord, You give me life! You have the words of eternal life,[65] Lord, You give me life! You are the Resurrection and the Life,[66] Lord, You give me life! You are the Way, the Truth and the Life, Lord You give me life![67]

---

[57] Ruth 4:14

[58] 1 Samuel 26:22-24

[59] 2 Samuel 4:9

[60] 1 Kings 3:14

[61] 1 Kings 17: 21-22

[62] 2 Kings 4:32

[63] John 6:35

[64] John 6:68

[65] John 11: 25

[66] John 14: 6

[67] John 14:6

Let Us Pray . . . Around the World Prayer Prompts

- International Workers
- The universal Church of Christ
- All those who lead the Church
- Leaders of the Nations
- The natural world and the resources of the Earth
- All who are in any kind of need
- The media and the arts
- Farmers and Fishers
- Commerce and industry
- Those whose work is unfulfilling, stressful or fraught with danger
- All who are unemployed
- Asia and its countries
- God's royal priesthood, that they may be empowered by the Spirit
- Those who wait on God, that they may find renewal
- The earth, for productivity and for fruitful harvests
- All who are struggling with broken relationships
- The saints on earth, that they may live as citizens of heaven
- All people, that they may hear and believe the Word of God
- All who fear the winter months
- All sovereigns and political leaders, that they may imitate the righteous rule of Christ
- All who grieve or wait with the dying
- Africa and its countries
- Homeless people
- Families with young children
- All who are lonely
- All who are near to death
- All who are facing loss
- The people of God, that they may proclaim the risen Lord
- God's creation, that the peoples of the earth may meet their responsibility to care
- Those in despair and darkness, that they may find the hope and light of Christ

- Those in fear of death, that they may find faith through the resurrection
- Prisoners and captives
- Prisoners, refuges and homeless people
- Our homes, families, friends, and all whom we love
- Those whose time is spent caring for others
- Those who are close to death
- Those who have lost hope
- The worship of the Church
- The Church, especially in places of conflict
- The Holy Land, for peace and justice and reconciliation
- Refugees and asylum seekers
- Those living in poverty or under oppression
- Immigrant families
- Europe and its countries
- Local government, community leaders
- All who provide local services
- Schools, colleges, apprenticeship programs and universities
- Emergency and rescue organizations
- The King, members of parliaments, legislatures, councils and the armed forces
- Peace and justice in the world
- Those who work for reconciliation
- All whose lives are devastated by war and civil strife
- Oceania Area and its countries
- Those who are enslaved
- The unity of the Church
- Peace in the world
- The healing of the sick
- The revelation of Christ to those from whom His glory is hidden
- All who travel
- Those preparing for spiritual rites of passage
- Those who are mislead by the false gods of this present age
- All who are hungry
- The persecuted Church
- The oppressed and colonized people of the world
- North and Central America and those countries

- All who are sick in body, mind, or spirit
- Those in the midst of famine or disaster
- Victims of abuse and violence, intolerance and prejudice
- Those who are bereaved
- All who work in the medical, health care and healing professions
- The social services workers
- Victims and perpetrators of crime
- The work of aid and relief agencies throughout the world
- Special States, Dependent Territories, Limited Recognition States
- My immediate family members
- My extended family members
- My neighbours
- My friends and families of friends
- Friends, family, and others with special needs
- My co-workers, colleagues, fellow students
- Churches (local and around world)
- Pastor(s), priest(s) and their families
- Church congregations
- Particular ministries:
- Particular region of world:
- Particular event(s):
- My personal needs:
- Missionaries and international workers
- Mid-Eastern countries
- Spiritual renewal and a deep sense of repentence
- Readiness to give a reason for the hope within us
- The flourishing of Christ's church everywhere
- Our capacity to serve the common good
- South America and its countries
- Those serving in leadership
- All who work in the criminal justice and correction systems
- Indigenous peoples who are at the margins of society
- Racial reconciliation
- Emerging generation
- Employment of those seeking work

- Those seeking asylum, refuge status, and escape from life-threatening places
- Deep missional identity in local churches
- Creative new conversation, environment and sustainability technologies
- Prisoners of conscience and emboldened advocates for justice
- Capacity to see and savour the wonder, beauty and complexity of creation
- Rights, best interests, and well-being of children, especially vulnerable children
- Effective teaching and preaching of God's Word
- Equipping for those working in the public arena, through elected roles
- Wise stewardship of physical resources
- Grace of asking forgiveness and for the boldness to confront wrong doing
- Muscians and artists who colour our world and fill our hearts with delight
- Eyes to see God's work in the world
- Members of gangs, crime communities, and tribes at war
- Those who are reminding us that we only have one planet, so we should smarten up
- A renewal of interest and commitment to serve the common good
- Those working in the news media
- Those trapped in prostitution, the sex industry; for drug dealers, and vice-advocates
- Deep involvement of local churches in the needs around them
- Deep and growing gratitude for the cross of Jesus Christ and His healing promises
- Safety of those who work in dangerous places or with dangerous substances
- The three or four countries in the world that might otherwise be ignored, even unknown

- Our stepped up efforts to reduce, reuse, and recycle
- Downfall of Satan and his despicable cohorts
- Uncovering of false and useless idols in our hearts
- For the lonely, abandoned, disenfranchised, cheated and exploited
- Fellowship with the risen Jesus Christ and for an abiding wonder at His sacrifice
- A deep awakening to the Gospel message amongst the apparently cold and disaffected
- A yearning to know God and the diligence to seek Him
- Those looking for forgiveness
- Church leaders

NOTES

Let Us Pray through the Psalms

Reading: Psalms 1 ☐ ☐
2 ☐ ☐ **3** ☐ ☐ **4** ☐ ☐

Let Us Pray . . .

O Triune God, Father, Son and Spirit, this morning, I welcome Your new mercies and Your promised presence in my life. Refresh my soul and remind me of Your abiding love. I know I was made by You and for You. Let this day's adventures begin. I want so much to be like a tree firmly planted by the streams of water, tended by You, and to bear fruit when ready. Keep me from fading and wilting but in all I am and in all I do, please mature and prosper me.[68]

I want to live as a person set apart for Your purposes and forever experience Your love, heed Your ways and know You are waiting for me to follow Your calling. I have peace when I go to bed, sleep and wake up in the morning because of Your safe-keeping and a confident trust. I know that You have set me apart for Yourself. You listen and heed when I call to You.[69]

Your love gives me immense joy and strength as I head into this new day. Live fully in me today Lord - so that the life I live - is explained by Your living in and through me. Please walk in my shoes, think through my mind and love through my personality. Please go before me, undergird, surround, oversee and walk beside me.

Lord I ask that You stand behind me today when I'm on the right track and provide me with boldness and energy, enabling me to make a modest but positive difference in this world. I ask that You block my way when I'm being foolish or on the brink of doing anything harmful. If I should get lost or distracted amid the complexities and perplexities of life, show me the way. And when there is too much hurry in my pace or my to-do

---

[68] Psalm 1:3 (Amplified Version)

[69] Psalm 4:3 (Amplified Version)

list is over-full, please reach out to me, gracious Lord, and bring me back into the quiet of Your presence and attune me with Your purposes. You, O Lord, are a shield for me, my glory, and You are the lifter of my head. I cry to You as I come into Your presence, You hear me, You answer me – I am in awe of Your attention.[70]

I acknowledge that each milisecond of the next 24 hours is known by You and held in Your care. I am assured, by the trustworthiness of Your character and the authority of Your Word, that nothing that happens or doesn't happen today can separate me from You and Your love. Lord, only You know what this day will bring my way. My life is altogether safe in Your hands and so I surrender my will to You for each moment of this day. Let me rest assured in that peace, the peace that only You can give.

Eternal God, grant to me, and those I dearly love, this day and every day, a readiness and delight in following Christ. Make me more teachable and more inwardly changeable. Whether the gift of this life is short or long, I will do all I can to live abundantly and in the power of Your Holy Spirit. Lord, be glorified in and through my life this day. Hear my prayer, O Lord. Gracious Father, receive these expressions as my prayer this morning and through the day - Give me, O Lord, a steadfast heart which no unworthy affection may drag downwards. Give me an unconquered heart which no tribulation can wear out. Give me an upright heart that no unworthy purpose may tempt aside. Bestow upon me also, O Lord my God, understanding to know You, diligence to seek You, wisdom to find You, and a faithfulness that may finally embrace You; through Jesus Christ our Lord.[71]

---

[70] Psalm 3: 3, 4 (Amplified Version)

[71] Last stanza adapted from Thomas Aquinas

Reading: Psalms 5 ☐ ☐ 6 ☐ ☐ 7 ☐ ☐

Let Us Pray . . .

O Lord, my God, thank You for bringing this day to a close; thank You for the anticipation and gift of rest for body and soul. Today Your hand has undergirded, guarded and preserved me. Thank You for giving me Your full attention. I am sorry for giving You much less of mine. Forgive my lack of faith and any wrong that I have done today, and help me to forgive all who have wronged me. Let me sleep in peace under Your protection, and keep me from all the temptations of darkness. Into your hands I commend my loved ones and all who dwell in this place; I commend to You my body, mind, soul and spirit. O God, Your holy name be praised.[72] Lord hear my supplications; Lord receive my prayer.[73] Almighty God, I want to be alert and responsive to every word and circumstance You provide for my service for you. Please keep my heart turned to You.

Continue to lift Your face upon me as I work and wait for You; resting beneath Your smile, Lord Jesus, earth's dark shadows flee. Brightness of my Father's glory, sunshine of my Father's face, let Your glory shine on me, fill me with Your grace.[74] In darkness and in light, in trouble and joy, help me, heavenly Father, to trust Your love, to serve Your purposes and to praise Your name, through Jesus Christ our Lord.[75]

But let all those of us who take refuge and put our trust in You rejoice; let me ever sing and shout for joy, because You cover me and defend me; let those of us who love Your name be joyful in You and be in high spirits. For You, Lord, will bless those who are upright and who are in right standing with You; as with a shield You surround me with

---

[72] Adapted from Dietrich Bonhoeffer
[73] Psalm 6:9 (Amplified Version)
[74] Jean Sophia Pigott, 19th Century
[75] Revised and adapted from The Daily Office

goodwill and Your favour.[76]

Almighty One! I bend in dust before You; in calm and still devotion I adore You, all wise, all present Friend! Here, leaning on Your promises leaning on Your strength may I be found. O, let my heart be ever Yours, until it ceases to beat! Be my portion, till we meet – face to face![77]

In holy contemplation, I sweetly pursue the theme of Your salvation, and find it ever new: Set *free from* present sorrow, I cheerfully can say, *Let the unknown morrow bring with it what it may.* It can bring with it nothing, but You will bear me through; You, who gives the lilies clothing, will clothe Your people too.[78] Jesus, I am resting, resting in the joy of who You are, I am finding out the greatness of Your loving heart. Here I gaze and gaze upon You, as Your beauty fills my soul, for by Your transforming power, You have made me whole.

Lord, help me to live this evening, quietly, easily; to lean on Your great strength, trustfully, restfully; to wait for the unfolding of Your will, patiently, serenely, joyfully; to face tomorrow, confidently, courageously.

I give thanks to You Lord for your rightness and justice, and I sing praise to Your name, Lord Most High.[79] Please listen to my words, O Lord, give attention to my deep sighing. Hear the sound of my cry, my King and my God, to You alone I pray. In the morning You hear my voice, O Lord; in the morning I will watch and wait for You to speak to my heart.[80] In peace I will lie down and sleep, for You, Lord, alone make me dwell in safety and confident trust.[81]

---

[76] Ps. 5:11, 12 (Amplified Version)

[77] Sir John Bowring, 1792-1872

[78] William Cowper, 1731-1800

[79] Psalm 7:17 (Amplified Version)

[80] Psalm 5:1, 2, 3 (Amplified Version)

[81] Psalm 4:8 (Amplified Version)

Reading: Psalms 8 ☐ ☐ 9 ☐ ☐ 10 ☐ ☐ 11 ☐ ☐

Let Us Pray . . .

I will praise You, O Lord, with my whole heart; I will recount and speak aloud of all Your marvelous works and wonderful deeds! I will rejoice in You and be in high spirits. Throughout this day, I will sing praise to Your name, O Most High![82] You note all trouble and grief; You are the helper of the fatherless.[83] Lord, You are righteous and love righteous deeds; the upright will behold Your face.[84]

Our Father in heaven, may Your name be kept holy. May Your Kingdom come soon. May Your will be done on earth, as it is in heaven. Give me today the food I need, and forgive me my sins, as I have forgiven those who sin against me. And don't let me yield to temptation, but rescue me from the evil one.[85]

Grow my sensitivity to and discernment of all that happens around me. As much as possible, please let me see the world, people and events as You see each. May I have a part in the answered prayer for more compassion and justice in this world. Today, by Divine appointment, may someone benefit from my service, offered as if unto You. Lord I have a genuine desire to be a help to someone today. Open my eyes to see who this will be. Delight me with the opportunity to be Your instrument of well-being in someone's life. Dear Jesus, lead me to someone this week with whom I can share the joy of Your fellowship, a kindred thirsty spirit with whom I can share support and encouragement.

O God, enlarge within me the sense of fellowship with all living things, my brothers the animals to whom You gave the earth as their home

---

[82] Psalm 9:1, 2 (Amplified Version)

[83] Psalm 10:14 (Amplified Version)

[84] Psalm 11:7 (Amplified Version)

[85] Matthew 6:9-13 (New Living Translation)

in common with us all. We remember, with shame, that in the past we humans have exercised the stewardship of high dominion with ruthless cruelty so that the voice of the earth, which should have gone up to You in song, has been a groan of travail. May I join with others in the realization that they live not for us alone but for all things living and, especially, for You, our Creator. May I, too, love the sweetness of life.[86]

O LORD, my Lord, how excellent and majestic is Your name in all the earth! You have set Your glory above the heavens. O Lord, how glorious is Your name in all the earth![87]

Jesus, You are the Joy of loving hearts, You are the Fount of life, You are the Light of humankind, from the best bliss that earth imparts I turn unfilled to You again. Your truth unchanged has ever stood; You save those who on You call: to those who seek You, You are good, to those who find You, all in all. I taste You, O You my living Bread, and long to feast upon You still; I drink of You, the Fountainhead, and thirst my soul from You to fill. My restless spirit yearns for You, where ever my changeful lot is cast, when Your gracious smile I see, blest when my faith can hold You fast. O Jesus, ever with me stay; make all my moments calm and bright; chase the dark night of sin away; shed o'er the world Your holy light.[88]

To You be the glory, now and forever. Amen

---

[86] Basil the Great, c.330-379

[87] Psalm 8:9 (Amplified Version)

[88] Bernard of Clairvaux, 1091-1153 (Tr. Ray Palmer, 1808-1887)

Reading: Psalms 12 ☐ ☐ 13 ☐ ☐ 14 ☐ ☐ 15 ☐ ☐

Let Us Pray . . .

Let my prayer be set forth in Your sight as incense, the lifting up of my hands as the evening sacrifice.[89] Heavenly Father I pray for grace and peace for myself and all those given to me to love.[90] I chose to worship You Lord, in the beauty of Your holiness; I join with the whole earth to tremble with reverence before You.[91]

O God, by whom the meek are guided in judgment, grant that the spirit of wisdom may guide me from all false choices, and that walking in Your straight path I may not stumble or fall.[92] Father, my Father! Send the Spirit of Your Son into my heart.[93] God be in my head, and in my understanding; God be in my eyes, and in my looking; God be in my mouth, and in my speaking; God be in my heart, and in my thinking; God be at my end, and at my departing.[94]

Speak to my heart as I silently wait on You O Lord, my Redeemer . . . I have leaned on and been confident in Your mercy and loving-kindness; my heart rejoices in Your salvation. I will sing to You Lord, because You have dealt bountifully with me.[95] May I be apart of a community of people who thirst after you – who praise You with the same and better gratitude I have for all You have done and continue to do in my life and in the lives of those I love. My soul continues to magnify the Lord Most High!

I confess my emptiness and weariness with meaninglessness; now fill me with "good things" through Jesus Christ, my Lord. My God, my God, let me for once look on You, as though nothing else existed but we alone! And as creation

---

[89] Psalm 141:2

[90] Philippians 1:2
[91] Psalm 96:9
[92] William Bright
[93] Galatians 4.6 (Good News Bible)

[94] Source unknown (found in Pynson's Horae, 1514)

[95] Psalm 13: 5, 6 (Amplified Version)

crumbles, my soul's spark expands till I can say *Even for myself I need You and I feel You and I love You.*[96] May Your Spirit guide my mind, which is so often dull and empty. Let my thoughts always be on You, and let me see You in all things. May Your Spirit enliven my soul, which is so often listless and lethargic. Let my soul be awakened to Your transforming presence, and let me know You in all things. May Your Spirit melt my heart, which is so often cold and indifferent. Let my heart be warmed by Your love, and let me feel You in all things.[97] Lord, You are in me but I am not near You till I have found You. Nowhere need I run to seek You, but You are already within me. You are the treasure hidden within me: draw me to You that I may find You and serve and possess You for ever.[98]

God, of Your goodness give me Yourself, for You are sufficient for me. I may not ask for anything less than what befits my full worship of You. If I were to ask anything less I should always be in want, for in You alone do I have all.[99]

Loving God, I offer these prayers, joining my voice to the great chorus of those who sing Your praise and depend on You alone. I long for the day when all Your children and creatures will live in Your peace and praise Your name. Until that day, give me sturdy patience and enduring hope, rooted only in Jesus, in whose name I pray. Amen

---

[96] Robert Browning, 1812-89

[97] Johann Freylinghausen, 1670-1739

[98] Walter Hilton, 14th century (adapted)

[99] Julian of Norwich, 1342-c.1416

Reading: Psalms 16 ☐ ☐ 17 ☐ ☐ 18:1-15 ☐ ☐

Let Us Pray . . .

You have invited me into Your presence Almighty God. In response, I bow in silence, remembering that my audience with You is possible through Jesus Christ - I come in His strong name. I come with a penitent and obedient disposition of heart to obtain forgiveness by confession of my sins and appropriating the benefits of Jesus' atoning sacrifice. I come without any merit on my own but, instead and entirely through His infinite goodness and mercy. "O God make speed to save me."

Our Father in heaven, hallowed be Your name, Your kingdom come, Your will be done on earth as it is in heaven. Give me today my daily bread. Forgive me my debts, as I also have forgiven my debtors. And lead me not into temptation, but deliver me from the evil one.[100]

Let me hear of Your steadfast love in the morning, for in You I put my trust. Teach me the way I should go, for to You I lift up my soul.[101] Most blessed Trinity, and one eternal God, as You have today woken me up from physical sleep, so wake up my soul from the sleep of sin; and as You have strengthened me through sleep, so after death give me life; for death to me is but to sleep with You, to whom be all glory, wisdom, majesty, dominion, and praise, now and always.[102] Lord, today I commit my energies to making this world a place where there is greater justice for all people — to pay attention to injustice and to act, as I am enabled to make a difference locally and globally. So help me Lord.

Bless me, today, Father, Son, and Holy Spirit, and

---

[100] Matthew 6:9-13 (New International Version)

[101] Psalm 143:8, 10 (New Revised Standard Version)

[102] Henry Vaughan

transform me through our friendship. Dear God, be good to me; for as others have said - the sea is so large, and my boat is so small. O Lord, in the morning You hear my voice; I offer myself to You and I volunteer to do whatever, go wherever, give up or take on whatever You will for me. Come fill my soul, Lord. As the dawn breaks into the sky; let Your sun rise in my heart at the coming of this new and precious day. Lord show me the path of life; for in Your presence is fullness of joy and at Your right hand there are pleasures forevermore.[103] Keep and guard me as the pupil of Your eye; hide me in the shadow of Your wings.[104] I love You fervently and devotedly, O Lord, my Strength. Lord You are my Rock, my Fortress, and my Deliverer; my God, my firm Strength in Whom I will trust and take refuge, my Shield, and the Horn of my salvation, my High Tower.[105]

O Lord my God, teach my heart where and how to seek You, where and how to find You. Lord, if You are not here but absent, where shall I seek You? But You are everywhere, so You must be here, why then do I not seek You? . . . Lord, I am not trying to make my way to Your height, for my understanding is in no way equal to that, but I do desire to understand a little of Your truth which my heart already believes and loves. I do not seek to understand so that I may believe, but I believe so that I may understand; and what is more, I believe that unless I do believe I shall not understand.[106]

O God, in Your loving purpose answer my prayers and fulfill my hopes. In all things for which I pray, give me the will to seek to bring them about, for the sake of Jesus Christ. Amen.

---

[103] Psalm 16:11 (Amplified Version)

[104] Psalm 17:8 (Amplified Version)

[105] Psalm 18:1, 2 (Amplified Version)

[106] Anselm, 1033-1109

Reading: Psalms 18:16-end ☐ ☐ 19 ☐ ☐

Let Us Pray . . .

Let the words of my mouth and the meditations of my heart be acceptable in Your sight, O Lord, my Rock and my Redeemer.[107]

Yours is the day, O God, yours also the night; You established the moon and the sun. You fixed all the boundaries of the earth; You made both summer and winter.[108]

Your ways are perfect! Your word is tested and tried; You are a shield to all those who take refuge and put their trust in You.[109] I will bless You Lord, for You have given me counsel; through my heart You teach me, night after night. I have set You as Lord of Lords always before me; because You are at my right hand, I shall not fall.[110]

For Lord, my God, You cause my lamp to be lit, to shine and to illuminate my darkness.[111] I seek You who made every constellation in the sky, and turns deep darkness into the morning, and darkens the day into night; who calls for the waters of the sea and pours them out upon the surface of the earth: The Lord is Your name.[112]

O Lord, deprive me not of Your heavenly blessings; O Lord, deliver me from eternal torment; O Lord, if I have sinned in my mind or thought, in word or deed, forgive me. O Lord, deliver me from every ignorance and inattention, from a petty soul and a stony, hard heart. O Lord, deliver me from every temptation; O Lord, lighten my heart darkened by evil desires. O Lord, I, being a human being, have sinned; You, being God, forgive me in Your loving kindness, for You know the weakness of my soul. O Lord, send down

---

[107] Psalm 19:14 (Amplified Version)
[108] Psalm 74:15,16
[109] Psalm 18:30 (Amplified Version)
[110] Psalm 16:7,8

[111] Psalm 18:28 (Adapted Amplified Bible)
[112] Amos 5:8

Your grace to help me, that I may glorify Your holy name. O Lord Jesus Christ, write my name, the name of Your servant, in the Book of Life, and grant me a blessed end. O Lord my God, even if I have done nothing good in Your sight, yet grant me Your grace, that I may make a start doing good.

O Lord, sprinkle on my heart the dew of Your grace; O Lord of heaven and earth, remember me, Your sinful servant, with my cold and impure heart, in Your kingdom. O Lord, receive me in repentance; O Lord, do not leave me. O Lord, save me from temptation; O Lord, grant me pure thoughts. O Lord, grant me tears of repentance, remembrance of death, and the sense of peace. O Lord, make me remember to confess my sins. O Lord, grant me humility, love, and obedience. O Lord, grant me tolerance, magnanimity, and gentleness. O Lord, implant in me the root of all blessings: the reverence of You in my heart. O Lord, grant that I may love You with all my heart and soul, and that I may obey Your will in all things; O Lord, shield me from evil people, devils and passions. O Lord, You know Your creation and what You have planned for it; may Your will also be fulfilled in me, a sinner, for You are blessed forever more. Amen.[113]

Almighty God have mercy on me, forgive me of all my sins. Through the Lord Jesus Christ, strengthen me in all goodness, and by the power of the Holy Spirit keep me in eternal life. O God, make speed to save me, and all those with whom I have relationships. O Lord, make haste to help me. Glory to the Father, and to the Son, and to the Holy Spirit: as it was in the beginning, is now, and will be forever. Amen and Alleluia.

---

[113] Chrysostom, according to the hours of the day and night

Reading: Psalms 20 ☐ ☐ 21 ☐ ☐

Let Us Pray . . .

My God, I give You this day. I offer You, now, all of the good that I shall do and I promise to accept, for love of You, all of the difficulty that I shall meet. Help me to conduct myself during this day in a way that pleases You.[114] Almighty God, You have promised to hear the petitions of those who ask in Your Son's Name: I ask that You mercifully incline Your ears to these prayers and supplications; and grant that those things, which I have faithfully asked according to Your will, may be obtained, to the relief of necessity, and to the setting forth of Your glory; through Jesus Christ the Lord.[115] I know that You O Lord save Your anointed; You will answer me from Your holy heaven with the saving strength of Your right hand.[116] Be exalted, Lord, in Your strength; we will sing and praise Your power.[117] Renew within me a vision and excitement by a sense of being on mission for You and Your lofty Kingdom purposes.

Our Father in heaven, hallowed be Your name. Your kingdom come, Your will be done, on earth as it is in heaven. Give me this day my daily bread and forgive me my debts, as I also have forgiven my debtors. And lead me not into temptation, but deliver me from evil.[118] Loving Father God, Your plans for me this week are superior to what I might invent for myself. Keep me open to Your plans and wary of those I make up, mimic or succumb to from others. I want to walk with confidence in Jesus Christ. I yield my life today to the filling of Your Spirit. I know the human spirit fails unless the Holy Spirit fills, so please fill me afresh.

---

[114] Francis de Sales

[115] Book of Common Prayer, 1549, Post-communion collect

[116] Psalm 20:6 (Adapted Amplified Bible)

[117] Psalm 21:13 (Adapted Amplified Bible)

[118] Matthew 6:9-13 (English Standard Version)

You have given me the run of the land, the pick of the crop and I, with others, have squandered these resources; distributed them unfairly, vandalized their beauty, violated their purity. Forgive me God, that I have taken Your kingdom for granted. You have given me the seeds of faith, the fruit of the Spirit, and I have misused these resources and this gift; displayed them too rarely, bestowed them grudgingly, ignored them blithely.

Thank you God that You are stronger than the worst of my destructiveness and greater than subtlest of my meanness. You give Me a fresh start, a second chance. Overwhelm me with the power of Your resurrected love. Compel me with the challenge You issue for change. Lead me in the conquest of my own limits and restrictions. Drive me towards a new life of justice, peace and integrity.[119] And help me, this day and every day, to live more nearly as I pray.[120] O Lord, forgive what I have been, sanctify what I am, and order what I shall be.[121]

Make me remember, O God, that every day is Your gift and ought to be used according to Your command, through Jesus Christ our Lord.[122]

O heavenly Father, in whom I live and move and have my being, I humbly pray for You to so guide and govern me by Your Holy Spirit, that in all the cares and occupations of my daily life I may never forget You, but remember that I am walking in Your sight; for Your name's sake.[123]

O Lord, support me all the day long, until the shadows lengthen, and the evening comes, and the busy world is hushed, and the fever of life

---

[119] Janet Orchard

[120] John Keble

[121] Author unknown

[122] Dr. Johnson

[123] An ancient collect

is over, and my work is done. Then, Lord, in Your mercy grant me a safe lodging, and a holy rest, and peace at the last; through Jesus Christ our Lord.[124]

Almighty God, in giving humankind dominion over things on earth, You made us fellow workers in Your creation. Give me and give us wisdom and reverence so to use the resources of nature that no one may suffer from my abuse of them, and that generations yet to come may continue to praise You for Your bounty, through Jesus Christ our Lord.[125]

Come, for You are Yourself the desire that is within me. Come, the consolation of my humble soul. Come, my Joy, my Endless Delight.[126]

Examine me, O Lord, and prove me, test my heart and my mind. For Your lovingkindness is ever before my eyes, and I seek to walk faithfully in Your truth.[127] This day will afford many opportunities to trust in You. Lord, make me see Your glory in every place.[128] My Lord and my God, take me from all that keeps me from You. Grant me all that leads me to You. Take me from myself and give me completely to You.[129]

Lord, give us weak eyes for things which are of no account and clear eyes for all Your truth.[130] Almighty God, bestow on me the meaning of words, the light of understanding, the nobility of diction and the faith of the true nature. And grant that what I believe I may also speak.[131]

---

[124] Used by J. Newman, based on a sixteenth-century prayer

[125] Episcopal Church of the United States of America. *Book of Common Prayer*

[126] Symeon the New Theologian, 949-1022

[127] Psalm 26:2, 3 (Adapted Amplified Bible)

[128] Michelangelo, 1475-1564

[129] Nicholas of Flue, 1417-87

[130] Soren Kierkegaard

[131] Hilary

Reading: Psalms 22 ☐ ☐ 23 ☐ ☐ 24 ☐ ☐

Let Us Pray . . .

If I say, "Surely the darkness will cover me, and the light around me turn to night," darkness is not dark to You, O Lord; the night is as bright as the day; darkness and light to You are both alike.[132] But be not far from me, O Lord; O my Help, hasten to aid me![133] God, the Father of our Lord Jesus Christ, increase in me faith, truth and gentleness, and grant me part and lot among Your saints.[134] My spirit is dry within me because it forgets to feed on You.[135]

O gracious light, pure brightness of the ever-living Father in heaven, O Jesus Christ, holy and blessed! Now as I come again to the setting of the sun, I sing Your praises, O God: Father, Son, and Holy Spirit. You are worthy at all times to be praised by happy voices, O Son of God, O Giver of Life, and to be glorified through all the worlds. The earth is the Lord's, and the fullness of it, the world and those who dwell in it. Who is this King of glory? It is the Lord of hosts, He is the King of glory.[136]

Lord, teach me the art of patience while I am well, and enable me to use it when I am sick. In that day either lighten my burden or strengthen my back. Make me, who so often in my health has presumed on my own strength, to be strong in my sickness when I solely rely on your assistance.[137] Guide me, teach me, and strengthen me, O Lord, I call out to You, until I become such as You have me to be: pure, gentle, truthful, high minded, courteous, generous, able, dutiful and useful; for

---

[132] Psalm 139:10, 11
[133] Psalm 22:19 (Adapted Amplified Bible)
[134] Polycarp
[135] John of the Cross

[136] Psalm 24: 1, 10 (Adapted Amplified Bible)
[137] Thomas Fuller

Your honour and glory.[138] Jesus said, "I am the light of the world; whoever follows me will not walk in darkness, but have the light of life."[139] LORD, You are my Shepherd, You feed, guide, and shield me, I shall not lack for anything.[140]

O God, who for my redemption gave Your only begotten Son to the death of the cross, and by His glorious resurrection has delivered me from the power of the enemy: Grant that I might die daily to sin, that I may evermore live with Him in the joy of His resurrection, through the same Jesus Christ my Lord.[141]

O Lord God, in whom I live and move and have my very being, open my eyes that I may behold Your fatherly presence ever with me. Draw my heart to You with the power of Your love. Teach me to be anxious for nothing, and when I have done what You give me to do, help me, O God my Saviour, to leave the issue to Your wisdom. Take from me all doubt and mistrust. Lift my heart up to You in heaven, and make me know that all things are possible to me through Your Son my Redeemer.[142]

I believe in God, the Father almighty, creator of heaven and earth. I believe in Jesus Christ, His only son, our Lord. He was conceived by the power of the Holy Spirit and born of the Virgin Mary. He suffered under Pontius Pilate, was crucified, died, and was buried. He descended to the dead. On the third day He rose again. He ascended into heaven, and is seated at the right hand of the Father. He will come again to judge the living and the dead. I believe in the Holy Spirit, the holy catholic Church, the communion of saints, the forgiveness of sins, the resurrection of the body, and the life everlasting. Amen.[143]

---

[138] Charles Kingsley

[139] John 8:12

[140] Psalm 23:1 (Adapted Amplified Bible)

[141] Gregorian Sacramentary

[142] Brooke Foss Westcott, 1825-1901

[143] The Apostles' Creed

Reading: Psalms 25 ☐ ☐ 26 ☐ ☐

Let Us Pray . . .

Holy Spirit, help me, weak as I am; I do not know how I ought to pray. See into my heart, and plead for me in groans that words cannot express.[144] Take a look Lord, an empty vessel that needs to be filled. My Lord, fill me. I am weak in the faith, strengthen me. I am cold in love; warm me and make me fervent so that Your love goes out to my neighbours. O Lord, help me. Strengthen my faith and trust in You. With me, there is an abundance of sin; in You is the fullness of righteousness. Therefore I will remain with You, from whom I can receive, but to whom I have only myself to give.[145] Lord, here I am, do with me as seems best in Your eyes; only give me, I ask You, a penitent and patient spirit to expect You. Make my service acceptable to You while I live, and my soul ready for You when I die.[146]

God, I feel flabby in my faith these days. While I pray You'd keep my family, friends and colleagues safe, I offer myself to You for the exercise entailed in Your bold Kingdom purposes. Lead me into interactions, relationships, responsibilities and situations that will increase the spiritual muscle tonus in me. I want to serve You exceptionally well. Father in heaven, hallowed be Your name. Your kingdom come. Your will be done, on earth as it is in heaven. Give me this day my daily bread. And forgive me my debts, as I also have forgiven my debtors. And do not lead me into temptation, but deliver me from evil. For Yours is the kingdom and the power and the glory forever. Amen.[147]

---

[144] Romans 8.26-7 (Good News Bible, adapted)

[145] Martin Luther

[146] William Laud .

[147] Matthew 6:9-13 (New American Standard Version)

Pour into my heart, Almighty God, the pure serene light of Your truth, that I may avoid the darkness of sin, through Jesus Christ our Lord.[148]

O Love, O God, You created me, in Your love recreate me. O Love, You redeemed me, fill up and redeem for Yourself whatever part has fallen into neglect within me. O Love, O God, you made me Yours, as the blood of Christ purchased me, in Your truth sanctify me. O Love, O God, You adopted me as a daughter/son, after Your own heart-fashion and form me. O Love, You chose me as Yours not another's; grant that I may cling to You with my whole being. O Love, O God, You loved me first, grant that with my whole heart, and with my whole soul, and with my whole strength, I might love You. O Love, O God almighty, in Your love confirm me. O Love most wise, give me wisdom in the love of You. O Love most sweet, give me sweetness in the taste of You. O Love most dear, grant that I may live only for You. O Love most faithful, in all my tribulations, comfort and nourish me. O Love who is always with me, O Love most victorious, grant that I may persevere to the end in You.[149]

Lord, enfold me in the depths of Your heart; and there hold me, refine, purge, and set me on fire, raise me aloft, until my own and carnal self knows utter annihilation.[150]

Gracious God, accept these prayers offered in Jesus' name, and give me now the strength to wait patiently for Your answer, and to live faithfully in response to Your call, through Christ, my Lord.

---

[148] Ambrosian Manual

[149] Gertrude of Thuringen

[150] Pierre Teilhard de Chardin, 1881-1955

Reading: Psalms 27 ☐ ☐ 28 ☐ ☐ 29 ☐ ☐ 30 ☐ ☐

Let Us Pray . . .

Hear the voice of my supplication as I cry to You for help, as I lift up my hands toward Your Holy of Holies. You Lord are my Strength and my impenetrable Shield; my heart trusts in, relies on, and confidently leans on You, and I am helped; therefore my heart greatly rejoices, and with my song will I praise You.[151] I give to You the glory due to Your name; I worship You Lord in the beauty of holiness or in holy array.[152] And still, O Lord, to me impart an innocent and grateful heart.[153]

Most loving Father, who has taught me to dread nothing except the loss of You, preserve me from faithless fears and worldly anxieties, from corrupting passions and unhallowed love of earthly treasures; and grant that no clouds of this mortal life may hide me from the light of that love which is immortal and which You have shown to me in Your Son, Jesus Christ our Lord.[154]

Lord, I am blind and helpless, stupid and ignorant, cause me to hear; cause me to know; teach me to do; lead me.[155] God, give me the serenity to accept what cannot be changed; give me the courage to change what should be changed; give me the wisdom to distinguish one from the other. Living one day at a time; enjoying one moment at a time; accepting hardships as the pathway to peace; taking as You did, this sinful world as it is, not as I would have it; trusting that You will make things right if I surrender to Your will; that I may be reasonably happy in this life

---

[151] Psalm 28:2, 7 (Adapted Amplified Bible)

[152] Psalm 29:2 (Adapted Amplified Bible)

[153] S.T. Coleridge

[154] William Bright

[155] Henry Martyn

and supremely happy with You forever in the next.[156]

You have searched me, LORD, and You know me. You know when I sit and when I rise; You perceive my thoughts from afar. You discern my going out and my lying down; You are familiar with all my ways. Before a word is on my tongue You, LORD, know it completely. You hem me in behind and before, and You lay Your hand upon me. Such knowledge is too wonderful for me, too lofty for me to attain. Where can I go from Your Spirit? Where can I flee from Your presence? If I go up to the heavens, You are there; if I make my bed in the depths, You are there. If I rise on the wings of the dawn, if I settle on the far side of the sea, even there Your hand will guide me, Your right hand will hold me fast. If I say, "Surely the darkness will hide me and the light become night around me," even the darkness will not be dark to You; the night will shine like the day, for darkness is as light to You. For You created my inmost being; You knit me together in my mother's womb.

I praise You because I am fearfully and wonderfully made; Your works are wonderful, I know that full well. My frame was not hidden from You when I was made in the secret place, when I was woven together in the depths of the earth. Your eyes saw my unformed body; all the days ordained for me were written in Your book before one of them came to be. How precious to me are Your thoughts, God! How vast is the sum of them! Were I to count them, they would outnumber the grains of sand— when I awake, I am still with You. Search me, God, and know my heart; test me and know my anxious thoughts. See if there is any offensive way in me, and lead me in the way everlasting.[157]

---

[156] Attributed to Reinhold Niebuhr, also known as 'The Serenity Prayer'

[157] Psalm 139

Reading: Psalms 31 ☐ ☐ 32 ☐ ☐

Let Us Pray . . .

O Lord, the Scripture says, "There is a time for silence and a time for speech." Saviour, teach me the silence of humility, the silence of wisdom, the silence of love, the silence of perfection, the silence that speaks without words, the silence of faith. Lord teach me to silence my own heart that I may listen to the gentle movement of the Holy Spirit within me and sense the depths which are of God.[158] You are a hiding place for me; You, Lord, preserve me from trouble, You surround me with songs and shouts of deliverance. Selah [pause, and calmly think of that]![159] Father in heaven, let Your name be kept holy. Let Your kingdom come. Let Your will be done on earth as it is done in heaven. Give me my daily bread today. Forgive me as I forgive others. Don't allow me to be tempted. Instead, rescue me from the evil one.[160] Lord, I greet You, this happy morning; O Jesus, to You be all glory given; Word of the Father, now in flesh appearing! I come and adore You, Christ, my Lord!" Descend to me, I pray; cast out my sin, and enter in; O come to me, abide with me, My Lord Emmanuel Amen.[161]

Grant me, Lord, to know in weakness the strength of Your incarnation: in pain the triumph of Your passion: in poverty the riches of Your Godhead: in reproach the satisfaction of Your sympathy: in loneliness the comfort of Your continual presence: in difficulty the efficacy of Your intercession: in perplexity the guidance of Your wisdom; and by Your glorious death and

---

[158] *Source unknown, 16th century*

[159] Psalm 32:7 (Amplified Bible)

[160] Matthew 6:9-13 (God's Word Translation)

[161] Adapted from "O Come, All Ye Faithful" and Phillips Brooks, "O Little Town of Bethlehem"

resurrection bring me at last to the joy of seeing You face to face.[162]

Lord, my soul is deeply guilty of envy. I would prefer Your work not done than done by someone else other than myself. Dispossess me, Lord, of this bad spirit, and turn my envy into holy emulation; yes, make other peoples' gifts to be mine, by making me thankful to You for them.[163]

I asked You for strength, that I might achieve, I was made weak, that I might learn humbly to obey. I asked for health, that I might do greater things, I was given infirmity, that I might do better things. I asked for riches, that I might be happy, I was given poverty, that I might be wise. I asked for power, that I might have the praise of others, I was given weakness, that I might feel the need of You. I asked for all things, that I might enjoy life, I was given life, that I might enjoy all things. I got nothing that I asked for but everything that I had hoped for, almost despite myself, my unspoken prayers were answered. I am among all persons most richly blessed.[164]

Lord, keep this and all nations under Your care; and guide me and us in the way of justice and truth. Let Your way be known upon earth; Your saving health among all nations. O Lord, let not the needy be forgotten; nor the hope of the poor be taken away.

Remind me today that dry places of life hold promise, that despair need only be momentary, that the worst of scenarios have the potential to draw the best out of me and that darkness can never overcome the light, that Your hope in me can extinguished.

Let Your face shine on Your servant; save me for Your mercy's sake and in Your loving-kindness.[165]

---

[162] Author unknown

[163] Thomas Fuller

[164] A Soldier's Prayer, written by an anonymous confederate soldier in the US civil war

[165] Psalm 31:16 (Amplified Bible)

Reading: Psalms 33 ☐ ☐ 34 ☐ ☐

Let Us Pray . . .

Give me grace, Almighty Father, to address You with all my heart as well as with my lips. You are everywhere present: from You no secrets can be hidden. Teach me to fix my thoughts on You, reverently and with love, so that my prayers are not in vain, but are acceptable to You, now and always; through Jesus Christ my Lord.[166]

Heavenly Father, may Your Holy Spirit lead the rich nations to support the poor, and the strong nations to protect the weak; so that every nation may develop in its own way, and work together with other nations in true partnership for the promotion of peace and the good of all human kind; through Jesus Christ our Lord.[167] Lord I know that to sin is to break a bond, to destroy a relationship, to withdraw myself from my God and Father, and from Your love. I know that a sinful act is less important for the disorder it creates than for what it says about me as a person: Who am I? Who do I love? What is my attitude toward God?[168] For my sin I am truly sorry and turn from sin to You O God. Lord Jesus, may the fire of Your Holy Spirit consume in me all that displeases You, and kindle in my heart a burning zeal for the service of Your kingdom; through the Saviour Jesus Christ.[169]

God, my whims and wishes—are co-mingled with deeper desires and imaginings that have been implanted by Your Holy Spirit. Thank You for Your activity in my life – please pay attention to me when I forget to. Dearest Lord, teach me to be

---

[166] Jane Austen, 1775-1817

[167] Source unknown

[168] W J. Burghardt

[169] Ancient collect

generous; teach me to serve You as You deserve; to give and not count the cost, to fight and not heed the wounds, to toil and not seek for rest, to labour and not seek reward, except to know that I do Your will.[170] Jesus, confirm my heart's desire to work, and speak, and think for You. Still let me guard the holy fire, and still stir up Your gift in me.[171]

Our Father, You called me and saved me in order to make me like your Son, the Lord Jesus Christ. Day by day, change me by the work of Your Holy Spirit so that I may grow more like Him in all that I think and say and do, to His glory.[172] Grant, Lord God, that in the middle of all the discouragements, difficulties and dangers, distress and darkness of this mortal life, I may depend on Your mercy, and on this build my hopes, as on a sure foundation. Let Your infinite mercy in Christ Jesus deliver me from despair, both now and at the hour of death.[173]

My thoughts and prayers tonight are with the homeless, the weary, the over-worked, the unemployed, the hungry, people who suffer innocently, the refuges, those with mental unwellness and atypicality, those in strife, all suffering children, and those who are grieving. Bring peace, comfort and Your special and tailor-made love to each of these.

O taste and see that the Lord God is good! Blessed am I for I trust and take refuge in You.[174] The counsel of the Lord stands forever, the thoughts of Your heart through all generations.[175]

Let Your mercy and loving-kindness, O Lord, be upon me, in proportion to my waiting and hoping for You.[176]

---

[170] Ignatius Loyola

[171] Charles Wesley

[172] Soren Kierkegaard

[173] Thomas Wilson

[174] Psalm 34:8 (Amplified Version)

[175] Psalm 33:11 (Amplified Version)

[176] Psalm 33:22 (Amplified Version)

Reading: Psalm 35 ☐ ☐

Let Us Pray . . .

Grant me grace, almighty Father, so to pray as to deserve to be heard.[177] Create in me a clean heart, O God. Sustain me with Your Holy Spirit. O Lord, save Your people, and bless Your heritage. Govern me and lift me up forever. Day by day I magnify You; and I worship Your name forever, world without end. I will happily talk of Your righteousness, rightness, and justice, and of all my reasons for praising You all the day long.[178]

I give thanks to You, heavenly Father, through Jesus Christ Your dear Son, that You have protected me through the night from all danger and harm; and I call on You to preserve and keep me, this new day also, from all sin and evil; that in all my thoughts, words and deeds, I might serve and please You. In Your hands I commend my body and soul, and all that is mine. Let Your holy angel guard me and my family, that the wicked one may have no power over us.[179] Lord Jesus Christ, You are the splendour of eternal Light, remove from my heart the darkness of night. Drive the snares of the crafty enemy from me. Amen.[180]

I keep preferring the frivolous, the selfish and the unhelpful – draw me back to attending to Your Word to me, and to an acknowledgement of Your every moment presence with me. Grant, O Lord, that I maybe so ravished in the wonder of Your love that I may forget myself and all things; may feel neither prosperity nor adversity; may not fear to suffer all the pain in the world rather than be parted from You. O let me feel You more inwardly, and truly present with me than I am with myself, and make me

---

[177] Jane Austen, 1775-1817

[178] Psalm 35:28 (Amplified Bible)

[179] Martin Luther

[180] Mozarabic Psalter

circumspect in Your presence, my holy Lord.[181]

Lord, almighty God, Father of Your beloved and blessed Son Jesus Christ, through whom I have come to the knowledge of Yourself, God of angels, of powers, of all creation, of all the saints who live in Your sight, I bless you for judging me worthy of this day, this hour, so that in the company of the martyrs I may share the cup of Christ, Your anointed one, and so rise again to *eternal life* in soul and body, immortal through the power of the Holy Spirit. May I be received among the martyrs in Your presence today as a rich and pleasing sacrifice. God of truth, stranger to falsehood, You have prepared this and revealed it to me and now You have fulfilled Your promise.[182]

O love eternal, my soul needs and chooses You eternally. Oh, come Holy Spirit, and inflame my heart with Your love. To love or to die. To die and to love. To die to all other love in order to live in Jesus' love, so that I may not die eternally. But that I may live in Your eternal love. O Saviour of my soul, I eternally sing, *Live, Jesus. Jesus, I love. Live, Jesus, whom I love. Jesus, I love, Jesus who lives and reigns forever and ever. Amen.*[183]

Grant me, O Lord, to know that which is worth knowing, to love that which is worth loving, to praise that which can bear with praise, to hate what in Your sight is unworthy, to prize what to You is precious, and, above all, to search out and to do what is well-pleasing to You, through Jesus Christ our Lord.[184]

---

[181] Robert Leighton

[182] Polycarp, prayer he prayed as he was burned at the stake, c. 155

[183] Francis de Sales, concluding prayer in his book, Treatise on the Love of God

[184] Thomas a Kempis, c.1380-1471

Reading: Psalms 36 ☐ ☐ 37 ☐ ☐

Let Us Pray . . .

Lord, please make my uprightness and right standing with You go forth as the light, and may justice and right shine. I want now to be still and to rest in You; wait for You and patiently lean on You.[185] The Lord says: "Love the Lord your God with your whole heart." So tonight I ask, have I kept You, my God, in mind and put You first in my life? Or do I find myself caught up with material concerns? Have I worshipped You, my God, throughout this day and in every way? Have I respected Your name, or have I dishonored You in anger and carelessness? Have I prayed even when I didn't feel like it? Have I trusted You and taken seriously Your personal love and concern for me? Have I genuinely repented of my sins and accept Your free and gracious forgiveness?

One thing have I asked of the Lord, that will I constantly seek to dwell in the house of the Lord and be in Your presence all the days of my life; to behold and gaze upon Your delightful beauty and meditate, consider, and inquire of You in Your Holy temple.[186] Hear, O Lord, have mercy and be gracious to me! O Lord, be my helper![187]

Lord, I know not what I ought to ask of You. You only know what I need. You know me better than I know myself. O Father, give to Your child what I don't know to ask. Teach me to pray. Pray yourself in me.[188]

Eternal Father, source of life and light, whose love extends to all people, all creatures, all things: grant to me that

---

[185] Psalm 37:6-7 (Amplified Bible)

[186] Psalm 27:4 (Amplified Bible)

[187] Psalm 30:10 (Amplified Bible)

[188] F. Fenelon

reverence for life which becomes those who believe in You; lest I despise it, degrade it, or come callously to destroy it. Rather let me be a part with those who preserve it, serve it, and sanctify it, after the example of Your Son, Jesus Christ our Lord.[189] You see my every pretense, my fabrications, my feeble hypocrisy, and know me for what I am. Have mercy on me this evening and make me new in Jesus. *Amen*

Lord, may Your Word rule in my life and may I rejoice in it. Your glory be my aim, Your holy will be my choice. Your promises be my hope. Your providence be my guard. Your arm my strong support. May You, Yourself, be my great reward.[190] Lord God Almighty, shaper and ruler of all creatures, we pray that by Your great mercy and by the token of the holy cross You will guide me to Your will. Make my mind steadfast, strengthen me against temptation, and keep me from all unrighteousness. Shield me against my enemies, seen and unseen. Teach me to inwardly love You before all things with a clean mind and a clean body. For You are my Maker and Redeemer, my help and comfort, my trust and hope, for ever.[191]

Take my life, and let it be consecrated, Lord, to You; take my moments and my days, let them flow in ceaseless praise.[192] Your mercy and loving-kindness, O Lord, extends to the skies, and Your faithfulness to the clouds. Your righteousness is like the mountains of God, Your judgments are like the great deep. O Lord, You preserve humankind and beasts. How precious is Your steadfast love, O God! The children of this world take refuge and put their trust under the shadow of Your wings. For you are the fountain of life; in Your light I see light.[193]

O God, whose Son Jesus Christ cared for the welfare

---

[189] Robert Runcie
[190] Christopher Wordsworth
[191] King Alfred the Great
[192] Frances Ridley Havergal
[193] Psalm 36:5-9 (Amplified Bible)

of everyone and went about doing good; grant me the imagination and perseverance to create in this country and throughout the world a just and loving society for the human family; and make me an agent of Your compassion to the suffering, the persecuted and the oppressed, through the Spirit of Your Son, who shared the suffering of children, my pattern and my redeemer, Jesus Christ.[194]

Lord, You are close to those who are broken hearted and You save those who are crushed with sorrow for sin and are humbly and thoroughly penitent.[195]

My Heavenly Father in heaven, Hallowed be Your name. Your kingdom come and Your will be done in earth, as it is in heaven. Give me this day my daily bread. And forgive my debts, as I forgive my debtors. And lead me not into temptation, but deliver me and all those I love from evil: For Yours is the kingdom, and the power, and the glory, forever. Amen.[196]

Let my prayer be counted as incense before You, and the lifting up of my hands as an evening sacrifice.[197]

---

[194] Source unknown

[195] Psalm 34:18 (Amplified Version)

[196] Matthew 6:9-13 (King James Version)

[197] Psalm 141:2

Reading: Psalms 38 ☐ ☐ 39 ☐ ☐

Let Us Pray . . .

O be joyful in the Lord my soul; serve the Lord with gladness and come before His presence with a song. I know that You Lord are God; it is You who has made me and not me myself; it is true that I am one of Your chosen people and a sheep of Your pasture. I go on my way through Your gates with thanksgiving and into Your courts with praise; I am thankful to You and search for opportunities to speak good of Your Name. For You Lord are gracious; Your mercy is everlasting; and Your truth endures from generation to generation.[198]

Our Father, here I am, at Your disposal, Your child, to use me to continue Your loving the world, by giving Jesus to me and through me, to each other and to the world.[199] O Lord, I am Yours. Do what seems good in Your sight, and give me complete resignation to Your will.[200] Lord, what specific things might I do today that will engage Your will into action in my life? Amen.

God of all goodness, grant that I might desire ardently, to seek wisely, to know surely, and to accomplish perfectly Your holy will, for the glory of Your name.[201] Govern all by Your wisdom, O Lord, so that my soul may always be serving You according to Your will, and not as I desire. Do not punish me by granting what I want and ask, if it offends Your love. Let me die to myself, that I may serve You, let me live to You.[202]

Lord, help me to know my end and to appreciate the measure of my days-what it is; let me know and realize how frail I am and how transient is my stay here on earth. And now, Lord, what do I wait for and expect? My

---

[198] Traditional Jubilate Psalm 100
[199] Adapted from Mother Teresa
[200] David Livingstone
[201] Thomas Aquinas
[202] Teresa of Avila

hope and expectation are in You. Hear my prayer, O Lord, and give ear to my cry. For I am Your passing guest, a temporary resident.[203] Please don't forsake me O Lord; O my God, please do not be far from me. Make haste to help me, O Lord, my Salvation.[204] O Lord, to keep me this day without sin; O Lord,. have mercy upon me, have mercy upon us. O Lord, let Your mercy be upon me; as my trust is in You. O Lord, in You have I trusted; let me never be confounded.

Father in heaven, hallowed be Your name. Your kingdom come. Your will be done, as in heaven, so on earth. Give me this day my daily bread. And forgive my debts, as I also have forgiven my debtors. And bring me not into temptation, but deliver me from the evil one.[205]

My Lord, I have nothing to do in this world but to seek and serve You. I have nothing to do with my heart and its affections but to breathe after You. I have nothing to do with my tongue and pen but to speak to You and for You, and to make known Your glory and Your will.[206] Lord God, teach me the preciousness of prayer. Teach me the value of its hiddenness in my public life; its wastefulness in the world's eyes; its disregard for eloquence if my spirit can only groan. Let my prayers be filled with the enjoyment of You for Your name's sake and for none other.[207] O God, come to my assistance O LORD, come right away to help me in this new day.[208]

---

[203] Psalm 39:4, 7, 12 (Amplified Bible)

[204] Psalm 38:21-22 (Amplified Bible)

[205] Matthew 6:9-13 (American Standard Version)

[206] Richard Baxter

[207] John Bell (Iona Community)

[208] Psalm 70:1

Reading: Psalms 40 ☐ ☐ 41 ☐ ☐ 42 ☐ ☐ 43 ☐ ☐

Let Us Pray . . .

Holy Jesus, give me the gift and spirit of prayer.[209]

Teach me to pray often, that I may pray oftener.[210] More of Your presence, Lord, impart, more of Your image let me bear; erect Your throne within my heart, and reign without a rival there.[211]

Many, O Lord my God, are the wonderful works which You have done, and Your thoughts toward me are astonishly loving; no one can compare with You! If I should attempt to declare and speak of them, they are too many to be numbered. Please do not hold Your tender mercy from me, O Lord; let Your loving-kindness and Your truth continually preserve me![212] And as for me, You have upheld me in my integrity and set me in Your presence forever. Blessed be the Lord, the God of Israel, from everlasting and to everlasting, from this age to the next, and forever! Amen and Amen, so be it.[213]

O God, the life of all who live, the light of the faithful, and the strength of those who labour: I join others to thank You for the blessings of the day that is past, and humbly ask for Your protection through the coming night.

The Lord says: *Love one another as I have loved you.* I ask: Do I love my parents and brothers and sisters and try to create a happy home life? Or am I sometimes thoughtless or even cruel toward them? Am I fair and honest in my relationships? Or do I sometimes lie or act phony, or take unfair advantage of others by cheating or stealing? Am I contributing to the welfare of my school or workplace? Or do I ridicule people without trying to make things better? Do I respect the rights and

---

[209] Jeremy Taylor
[210] Jeremy Taylor
[211] John Newton
[212] Psalm 40:5, 11 (Amplified Bible)
[213] Psalm 41:12-13 (Amplified Bible)

sensitivities of others? Or am I prejudiced at times and tend to put people in categories or ignore them because they are different? Do I honestly try to forgive people who dislike me? Or have I tried to hurt them by what I've said or done? Am I grateful for my sexuality and anxious to grow in sexual maturity and responsibility? Or do I sometimes exploit members of the opposite sex and use their bodies? Am I trying to improve the quality of life around me? Or do I foul up the environment and waste the good things I have? Do I really care about my country and the good of the human community of which I am a part? Or do I care only about myself and the people I know? Am I concerned for the poor, the hungry and the destitute and for the millions who thirst for justice and peace? Can I cut back on excessive eating and drinking and contribute to the poor of the world? Examine my heart with these and other searching questions O Lord. Cleanse me as I lift my head, heart and hands to You.

Inpute Your righteousness to me through the atoning and finished work of Jesus Christ that I might be set apart for Your use and Your glory. Cleanse me, fill me, use me O God, my Redeemer, Sanctifier, Healer and Coming King.

In the same way a deer pants and longs for the clear, cool and flowing water brook, so I pant and long for You, O God. My inner self thirsts for God, for the living God.[214] Lord, You will command Your loving-kindness in the daytime, and in the night Your song shall be with me, a prayer to the God of my life.[215] O send out Your light and Your truth, let them lead me; let them bring me to Your holy hill and to Your dwelling.[216] I am Yours forever! To you, O Lord, I lift my soul. O God, in You I trust.[217]

---

[214] Psalm 42:1-2 (Amplified Bible)
[215] Psalm 42:8 (Amplified Bible)
[216] Psalm 43:3 (Amplified Bible)
[217] Psalm 25:1-2

Reading: Psalm 44 ☐ ☐ 45 ☐ ☐

Let Us Pray . . .

O God, early in the morning I cry to You. Help me to pray and to concentrate my thoughts on You; I cannot do this alone. In me there is darkness, but with You there is light. I am lonely, but You do not leave me. I am feeble in heart, but with You there is help. I am restless, but with You there is peace. In me there is bitterness, but with You there is patience. I do not understand Your ways, but You know the way for me.[218] O my God, may I always keep myself in Your love, by praying in the Holy Spirit. As Your infinite love is always streaming in blessings on me, so let my soul be always breathing love to You.[219]

My Father who is in heaven, hallowed be Your name. Your kingdom come. Your will be done on earth as it is in heaven. Give me and my family our daily bread today. And forgive us our debts, as we also forgive our debtors. And lead us not into temptation. But deliver us from evil. Amen.[220] There is a gaping sore, Lord: half the world diets, the other half hungers; half the world is housed, the other half homeless; half the world pursues profit, the other half senses loss. Redeem our souls, redeem our peoples, redeem our times.[221] Lord, may I be both mindful and obedient to my part in making a difference in this hurting world and in these times. Put Your compassion in my heart and lead me to be one of Your ambassadors and agents of reconciliation and hope in the world – I pray.

O Lord, You have mercy on all, take away from me my sins, and mercifully kindle in me the fire of your Holy Spirit. Take away from me the heart of stone, and give me a heart of flesh, a heart to

---

[218] Dietrich Bonhoeffer
[219] Thomas Ken
[220] Matthew 6:9-13 (Douay-Rheims Bible)
[221] John Bell (Iona Community)

love and adore You, a heart to delight in You, to follow and to enjoy You, for Christ's sake.[222] Give me a spirit of courage and a willingness to face Your truth, rely on Your love and accept Your full lordship over my surrendered life. Amen.

O Lord, the Scripture says, There is a time for silence and a time for speech: Saviour, teach me the silence of humility the silence of wisdom, the silence of love, the silence of perfection, the silence that speaks without words, the silence of faith. Lord, teach me to silence my own heart that I may listen to the gentle movement of the Holy Spirit within me and be aware of Your depths.[223]

Give me grace, O my Father, to be utterly ashamed of my own reluctance to pray. Rouse me from sloth and coldness, and make me desire You with my whole heart. Teach me to love meditation, sacred reading, and prayer. Teach me to love what which must engage my mind for all eternity.[224] I lean on You and ask for strength for the day. Please give me courage to displace my timidity; peace to replace my anxiety; encouraging nudges when I falter; a quickened sense of keeping short accounts with others and a clear sense of Your presence when I become discouraged.

O God, who makes me glad with the remembrance of the glorious resurrection of Your Son our Lord: Grant me this day such blessing through my worship of You, that the days to come may be spent in Your favour, through Jesus Christ my Lord. Amen. Your throne, O God, is forever and ever.[225] Come to my help, and deliver me for Your mercy's sake and because of Your steadfast love![226]

---

[222] Ambrose

[223] Source unknown, 16th century

[224] J.H. Newman

[225] Psalm 45:6 (Amplified Bible)

[226] Psalm 44:26 (Amplified Bible)

Reading: Psalms 46 ☐ ☐ 47 ☐ ☐ 48 ☐ ☐

Let Us Pray . . .

Almighty God, from whom every good prayer comes, deliver me, as I draw close to You, from coldness of heart and wanderings of mind, that with steadfast thought and kindled desire I may worship You in the faith and spirit of Jesus Christ our Lord.[227] Lord, teach me to seek You, and reveal Yourself to me as I seek you. For I cannot seek You unless You first teach me and I cannot find You unless You first reveal Yourself to me.[228]

Lord of hosts, You are with me; God of Jacob You are my Refuge, my Fortress and High Tower.[229] You, Lord Most High, excite terror, awe, and dread; You are the great King over all the earth.[230] Great are You Lord, and highly to be praised in the city of God! As is Your name, O God, so is Your praise to the ends of the earth; Your right hand is full of righteousness, rightness and justice.[231]

From moral weakness, from hesitation, from fear of humankind and dread of responsibility, strengthen me with courage to speak the truth in love and self-control. And alike from the weakness of hasty violence and from the weakness of moral discipline. From weakness of judgment, cowardice: Save and help me, O LORD.

From the indecision that can make no choice and from the irresolution that carries no choice into act, strengthen my eye to see and my will to choose the right. And from losing opportunities to serve You, and from perplexing myself and others with uncertainties: Save and help me, O LORD.

---

[227] William Bright, 1824-1901

[228] Ambrose of Milan

[229] Psalm 46:7 (Amplified Bible)

[230] Psalm 47:2 (Amplified Bible)

[231] Psalm 48:1, 10 (Amplified Bible)

From infirmity of purpose, from want or earnest care and interest, from sluggish indolence and slack indifference, and from all spiritual deadness of heart: Save and help me, O LORD.[232]

Lord, my heart is before You. I try, but by myself I can do nothing; do what I cannot. Admit me into the inner room of Your love. I ask, I seek I knock. You have made me seek, make me receive. You have enabled me to seek, enable me to find. You have taught me to knock, open to me. I faint with hunger for Your love, refresh me with it. Let me be filled with Your love, rich in Your affection, completely held in Your care. Take me and possess me wholly, who with the Father and the Holy Spirit are alone blessed from age to age.[233]

May Your compassion touch the disadvantaged, the disenfranchised, the forgotten, the embittered, the shut-in and the shut-up. Make me alert to the needs of those around me, I pray.

Come, Lord, work on me, set me on fire and clasp me close, be fragrant to me, draw me to Your love, let me run to You.[234]

Almighty God, my heavenly Father, without whose help labour is useless, without whose light search in vain, invigorate my studies and direct my enquiries, that I may through due diligence and right discernment establish myself and others in Your holy faith. Take not, O Lord, Your Holy Spirit from me, let not evil thoughts have dominion in my mind. Let me not linger in ignorance and doubt, but enlighten and support me for the sake of Jesus Christ the Lord.[235]

---

[232] From Southwell Litany

[233] Anselm, Meditation on Human Redemption

[234] Augustine

[235] Dr. Johnson

Reading: Psalm 49 ☐ ☐ 50 ☐ ☐

Let Us Pray . . .

O Holy One, teach me to pray, pray You Yourself in me.[236] Kick-start something new in and through me today, O God—Jesus Christ live fully in me this morning. Amen.

Almighty and most merciful Father, I have erred and strayed from Your ways like a lost sheep, I have followed too much the devices and desires of my own heart, I have offended against Your holy laws. I have left undone those things which I ought to have done, and I have done those things which I ought not to have done, and there is no health in me. But You, O Lord, have mercy upon me - a miserable offender; spare me, O God, as I confess my faults, restore me through my penitent heart, according to Your promises declared to humankind in Christ Jesus the Lord. And grant, O most merciful Father, for His sake, that I may from this day forward live a godly, righteous, and sober life, to the glory of Your holy Name.[237]

Our Father who is in heaven, hallowed be Your name in all the earth. Your kingdom come. Your will be done, as in heaven, so on earth. Give me this day my daily bread. And forgive my debts, as I also have forgiven my debtors. Forgive me my sins, O Lord, the sins of my present and the sins of my past, the sins of my soul and the sins of my body, the sins which I haved done to please myself and the sins which I have done to please others. Forgive me my casual sins and my deliberate sins, and those which I have tried to hide so that I have hidden them even from myself. Forgive me them, O Lord, forgive them all, for Jesus Christ's sake.[238] And bring me not into temptation, but

---

[236] Francois Fenelon, 1651-1715

[237] Book of Common Prayer, 1552, Morning and Evening Prayer

[238] Bishop Thomas Wilson

deliver me from the evil one.[239]

Almighty God, whose most dear Son first suffered pain and anguish before he was crucified: Mercifully grant that I, walking in the way of the cross, may find the way of life and peace, through your Son Jesus Christ our Lord. The Mighty One, God, the Lord, You speak and call the earth from the rising of the sun to its setting. You are the perfection of beauty, You shine forth.[240] God redeem me from the power of hell and receive me into the Kingdom of Your Son.[241]

Lord, help me to let go of any baggage from the past that hinders me and others. Help me to be open to new and generous ways of interacting today. Be merciful to me Lord.

If only I possessed the grace, good Jesus, to be utterly at one with you! Amidst all the variety of worldly things around me, Lord, the only thing I crave is unity with You. You are all my soul needs. Unite, Dear Friend of my heart, this unique little soul of mine to Your perfect goodness. You are all mine; when shall I be yours? Lord Jesus, my beloved, be the magnet of my heart; clasp, press, unite me forever to Your sacred heart. You have made me for Yourself; make me one with You. Absorb this tiny drop of life into the ocean of goodness where it came.[242]

Thanks be to God through my Lord Jesus Christ. Amen.

---

[239] Matthew 6:9-13 (English Revised Version)

[240] Psalm 50:1-2 (Amplified Bible)

[241] Psalm 49:15 (Amplified Bible)

[242] Francis de Sales, 1567-1622

Reading: Psalms 51 ☐ ☐ 52 ☐ ☐ 53 ☐ ☐ 54 ☐ ☐

Let Us Pray . . .

O Lord, hear my prayers, not according to the poverty of my asking but according to the richness of Your grace, so that my life may conform to those desires which accord with Your will; through Jesus Christ our Lord.[243] If I were to ask, I know there are many people who know me well and could suggest ways for me to improve my life. Instead, my strong preference is to have You assess my needs, forgive my sins, to unleash and empower me to be the person You created me to be. So help me Lord. Amen.

Have mercy on me, O God, according to Your steadfast love, according to Your abundant mercy blot out my transgressions. Wash me thoroughly from my iniquity, and cleanse me from my sin. For I know my transgressions, and my sin is ever before me. Against You, You alone, have I sinned, and done what is evil in Your sight, so that you are justified in Your sentence and blameless when you pass judgment .... Create in me a clean heart, O God, and put a new and right spirit within me. Do not cast me away from Your presence, and do not take Your Holy Spirit from me ... O Lord, open my lips, and my mouth will declare Your praise. For You have no delight in sacrifice; if I were to give a burnt offering, You would not be pleased. The sacrifice acceptable to God is a broken spirit; a broken and contrite heart, O God, You will not despise.[244]

Hatred which divides nation from nation, race from race, class from class, Father, forgive. Covetous desires of humankind and nations to possess what is not our own, Father, forgive. Greed which exploits the labours of persons, and lays waste the earth, Father, forgive. Envy of the welfare and happiness

---

[243] Reinhold Niebuhr, 1892-1971

[244] Psalm 51:1-4, 10-11, 15-17 (New Revised Standard Version)

of others, Father, forgive. Indifference to the plight of the homeless and the refugee, Father, forgive. Lust which uses for selfish ends the bodies of men and women, Father, forgive. Pride which leads me to trust in myself and not in You, Father, forgive.[245] Strengthen me, O God, to relieve the oppressed, to hear the groans of poor prisoners, to reform the abuses of all professions, that many not be made poor to make a few rich, for Jesus Christ's sake.[246]

Hover over those places of special need where there is human suffering, conflict and war. Penetrate those dark places with Your light that the world may achieve a new order and harmony under Your rule. Your Kingdom come, O Lord.

Make me worthy, Lord, to serve my fellow human beings throughout the world who live and die in poverty and hunger. Give them, through my hands, this day their daily bread; and by my understanding love, give peace and joy.[247]

I will thank You and confide in You forever, because You have delivered me and kept me safe. I will wait on, hope in and expect in Your name, for it is good, in the presence of Your saints.[248] Save me, O God, by Your name; judge and vindicate me by Your mighty strength and power. ²Hear my pleading and my prayer, O God; give ear to the words of my mouth.[249]

Deliver me and those I love, gracious God, from the powers of darkness through Your redeeming resurrection love. I pray in the name of the Risen One. Amen

---

[245] From Prayer on a plaque on the altar of Coventry Cathedral, written in 1964

[246] Oliver Cromwell, 1599-1658 (from a letter which he wrote after the Battle of Dunbar, 1650)

[247] Mother Teresa

[248] Psalm 52:9 (Amplified Bible)

[249] Psalm 54:1-2 (Amplified Bible)

Reading: Psalms 55 ☐ ☐ 56 ☐ ☐

Let Us Pray . . .

Our heavenly Father, who through Your Son Jesus Christ said that people ought always to pray and not to faint, I call on You, please teach me to pray. My spirit is willing but my flesh is weak. Give me grace each day to approach Your throne and seek Your face; to be concerned as much for Your glory as for my needs; and in everything by prayer and supplication with thanksgiving to make my requests known to You, until my life is gathered up into Your presence and every breath is prayer, through Jesus Christ Your Son, my ransom and mediator.[250]

O be joyful in the Lord my soul; serve the Lord with gladness and come before His presence with a song. I know that You Lord are God; it is You who has made me and not me myself; it is true that I am one of Your chosen people and a sheep of Your pasture. I go on my way through Your gates with thanksgiving and into Your courts with praise; I am thankful to You and will constantly speak well of Your name. For You Lord are gracious; Your mercy is everlasting; and Your truth endures from generation to generation.[251]

Almighty God, who after the creation of the world rested from all Your works and sanctified a day of rest for all Your creatures: Grant that I might put away all earthly anxieties, may be duly prepared for Your service on earth, and that Your willingness to be my Sabbath on earth may be a preparation for the eternal rest promised to Your people in heaven, through Jesus Christ our Lord. Amen.

O Lord, open my mind to see myself as you see me, and from all unwillingness to know my weakness and my sin, Good Lord, deliver me.

---

[250] John R. W. Stott

[251] Traditional Jubilate Psalm 100

From selfishness; from wishing to be the centre of attention; from seeking admiration; from the desire to have my own way in all things; from unwillingness to listen to others; from resentment of criticism, Good Lord, deliver me. From love of power; from jealousy; from taking pleasure in the weakness of others, Good Lord, deliver me. From the weakness of indecision; from fear of adventure; from constant fear of what others are thinking of me; from fear of speaking what I know is truth, and doing what I know is right, Good Lord, deliver me. From possessiveness about material things and people; from carelessness about the needs of others; from selfish use of time and money; from all lack of generosity, Good Lord, deliver me. From laziness of conscience; from lack of self-discipline; from failure to persevere; from depression in failure and disappointment, Good Lord, deliver me. From failure to be truthful; from pretence and acting a part; from hypocrisy; from all dishonesty with myself and with others, Good Lord, deliver me. From impurity in word, in thought, and in action; from failure to respect the bodies and minds of others and myself; from any kind of addiction, Good Lord, deliver me. From hatred and anger; from sarcasm; from lack of sensitivity and division in my communities; from all failure to love and to forgive, Good Lord, deliver me. From failure to see my sin as an affront to You, my God; from failure to accept the forgiveness of others, Good Lord, deliver me.[252]

O Father, my hope, O Son, my refuge, O Holy Spirit, my protection. Holy Trinity, glory to You.[253] Our Father in heaven, may Your name be kept holy. Let Your Kingdom come. Let Your will be done, as in heaven, so on earth. Give us today our daily bread. Forgive us our debts,

---

[252] Peter Nott

[253] Office of Compline, Eastern Orthodox Church

as we also forgive our debtors. Bring us not into temptation, but deliver us from the evil one. For Yours is the Kingdom, the power, and the glory forever. Amen.[254]

Father, give us wisdom to perceive You, intellect to understand You, diligence to seek You, patience to wait for You, eyes to behold You, a heart to meditate on You and a life to proclaim You, through the power of the Spirit of the Lord Jesus Christ.[255]

Eternal Light, shine into my heart; eternal Goodness, deliver me from evil; eternal Power, be my support; eternal Wisdom, scatter the darkness of my ignorance; eternal Pity, have mercy on me, that with all my heart and mind and strength I may seek Your face and be brought by Your infinite mercy into Your holy presence; through Jesus Christ the Lord.[256]

My Lord and my God, take me from all that keeps me from You. My Lord and my God, grant me all that leads me to You. My Lord and my God, take me from myself and give me completely to You.[257]

O God, surprise me today at work, invade my complacency with some fresh perspectives, insights and help me to be a part of a meaningful breakthrough. Amen.

---

[254] Matthew 6:9-13 (World English Bible)

[255] Benedict

[256] Alcuin

[257] Nicholas of Flue

Reading: Psalms 57 ☐ ☐ 58 ☐ ☐ 59 ☐ ☐ 60 ☐ ☐

Let Us Pray . . .

Holy Jesus, give me the gift and spirit of prayer; and by Your gracious intercession supply my ignorance, and passionate desires, and imperfect choices; procuring and giving me such returns of favour to support my needs, and serve the ends of religion and the Spirit, which Your wisdom chooses, and Your passion has purchased, and Your grace loves to bestow upon all Your saints and servants.[258] Have mercy on me, O God, according to Your steadfast love; according to all of Your tender mercy and loving-kindness blot out my transgressions. Wash me thoroughly and repeatedly from my iniquity and guilt. Cleanse me and make me wholly pure from my sin! For I am conscious of and do acknowledge my transgressions, my sin is ever before me. Against You, You only, have I sinned and done that which is evil in Your sight, so that You are justified in Your sentence and faultless in Your judgment. Purify me, and I shall be clean; wash me, and I shall be whiter than snow. Make me to hear joy and gladness and be satisfied; let the bones You have broken rejoice. Hide Your face from my sins and blot out all my guilt and iniquities. Create in me a clean heart, O God, and renew a right, persevering, and steadfast spirit within me. Please don't cast me away from Your presence and take not Your Holy Spirit from me. Restore to me the joy of Your salvation and uphold me with a willing spirit.[259]

As for me, I will call upon God, and You will save me. Evening and morning and at noon will I utter my complaint, moan and sigh,

---

[258] Jeremy Taylor, 1613-67

[259] Psalm 51:1-4, 7-12 (Amplified Bible)

and You will hear my voice.[260] I cast my burden on You Lord and I release the weight. You will sustain me.[261] In You have I put my trust and confident reliance; I will not be afraid. What can any human do to me? Your vows are upon me, O God; I will render praise to You and give You thanks. For You have delivered my life from death, and my feet from falling, that I may walk before God in the light of life and of the living.[262] O my Strength, I will watch and give heed to You and sing praises; for You are my Defense, my Protector, and my High Tower. My God in Your mercy and steadfast love meet me; I will sing of Your mighty strength and power; yes, I will sing aloud of Your mercy and loving-kindness in the morning; for You have been to me a defense and a refuge in the day of my distress. Unto You, O my Strength, I will sing praises; for God is my Defense, my Fortress, and my High Tower; my God who shows me mercy and steadfast love.[263]

From love of flattery, from over-ready belief in praise, from dislike of criticism, and from the comfort of self-deception in persuading myself that others think better of me than I am: Save and help me, O LORD. From all love of display and sacrifice to popularity, from thinking of myself and forgetting You in my worship: Hold my mind in spiritual reverence; and from self-glorification in all my words and works: Save and help me, O LORD. From pride and self-will, from the desire to have my way in all things, from overweening love of my own ideas, and blindness to the value of others, from resentment against opposition and contempt for the claims of others: Enlarge the generosity of my heart and enlighten the fairness of my judgments; and from all selfish arbitrariness of

---

[260] Psalm 55:16-17 (Amplified Bible)

[261] Psalm 55:22 (Amplified Bible)

[262] Psalm 56:10-13 (Amplified Bible)

[263] Psalm 59:9, 10a, 16, 17 (Amplified Bible)

tempter: Save and help me, O LORD.[264]

I will praise and give thanks to You, O Lord; I will sing praises to You among the nations. Your mercy and loving-kindness are great, reaching to the heavens, and Your truth and faithfulness to the clouds. Be exalted, O God, above the heavens; let Your glory be over all the earth.[265] You have set up a banner for those who fear and worshipfully revere You, a standard displayed because of the truth. Your beloved ones are delivered and saved with Your right hand when we call upon You.[266]

Grant, O Lord, that what I have said with my lips, I may believe in my heart and practise in my life; and of Your mercy keep me faithful to the end, for Christ's sake.[267] Come, O come Emmanuel. Amen

---

[264] From Southwell Litany

[265] Psalm 57:9-11 (Amplified Bible)

[266] Psalm 60:4-5 (Amplified Bible)

[267] John Hunter

Reading: Psalms 61 ☐ ☐ 62 ☐ ☐ 63 ☐ ☐

Let Us Pray . . .

Holy, holy, holy! Lord God Almighty! Early in the morning our song shall rise to You, Holy, holy, holy, merciful and mighty! God in three Persons, blessed Trinity! Holy, holy, holy! All the saints adore You, casting down their golden crowns around the glassy sea; cherubim and seraphim falling down before You, Who was, and is, and evermore shall be. Holy, holy, holy! Though the darkness hide You, though the eye of sinful humans Your glory may not see; only You are holy; there is none beside You, Perfect in power, in love, and purity. Holy, holy, holy! Lord God Almighty! All Your works shall praise Your Name, in earth, and sky, and sea; Holy, holy, holy; merciful and mighty! God in three Persons, blessed Trinity![268]

---

[268] Reginald Heber

O God, King eternal, who divides the day from the night and turns the shadow of death into the morning: Drive far from me all wrong desires, incline my heart to keep Your law, and guide my feet into the way of peace. O God, who is the author of peace and lover of order, in whose service is perfect freedom: Defend me, Your humble servant, in all assaults of my enemies; that I, trusting in Your defense, may not fear the power of any adversaries, through the might of Jesus Christ our Lord. Amen.

Look with pity, O heavenly Father, upon the people in this land who live with injustice, terror, disease, and death as their constant companions. Have mercy upon them, on us and on me. Help me to participate in the elimination of cruelty towards my neighbours. Strengthen those who spend their lives establishing equal protection of the law and providing opportunities for all. And grant that every man, woman, girl and boy in this country may enjoy a fair portion of the riches and benefits of this land, through Jesus Christ our Lord.[269]

Hear my cry, O God; listen to my prayer. From the end of the earth will I cry to You, when my heart is overwhelmed and fainting; lead me to the rock that is higher than I.[270] My God, for You alone my soul waits in silence; from You comes my salvation. You only are my Rock and my Salvation, my Defense and my Fortress, I shall be unshaken in Your care.[271] Because Your lovingkindness is better than life, my lips shall praise You. So will I bless You while I live; I will lift up my hands in Your name.[272]

Our Father in heaven, may Your name be kept holy. May Your kingdom come. May Your will be done, on earth as it is in heaven. Give me today my daily bread, and forgive me my sins, as I have forgiven those who have sinned against me. And never bring me into temptation, but deliver me from the evil one.[273] Lord, take what I am best at in my work, and set me into a disciplined alignment and attunement to Your purposes for me in this day.

Self-giving Lord, cause love to abound in and overflow from my life to the world. O Holy Saviour, cause me to serve You with joy and eager enthusiasm through this day – Your will be done. Amen

---

[269] Episcopal Book of Common Prayer
[270] Psalm 61:1-2 (Amplified Bible)
[271] Psalm 62:1-2 (Amplified Bible)
[272] Psalm 63:3-4 (Amplified Bible)

[273] Matthew 6:9-13 (International Standard Version)

Reading: Psalms 64 ☐ ☐
65 ☐ ☐ **66** ☐ ☐ **67** ☐ ☐

Let Us Pray . . .

Lord, teach me to pray often, that I may pray oftener.[274] Lord, if it had been a completely satisfactory and fully lived day I wouldn't bother praying tonight; but I've fallen short again. I need Your healing touch, Your reassuring presence, and Your unfailing friendship.

The righteous will be glad in You O Lord. I will trust and take refuge in You; and I will join with all the upright in heart to glorify and offer praise to You.[275] O You who hear prayer, to You will every person come. Iniquities and varied guilt prevail against me Lord; yet as for my transgressions, You forgive and purge them having made atonement for them and covering them from Your sight![276]

Lord Jesus Christ, You said that You are the Way, the Truth, and the Life. Help me not to stray from You, for You are the Way; nor to distrust You, for You are the Truth; nor to rest on any other than You, as You are the Life. You have taught me what to believe, what to do, what to hope, and where to take my rest. Give me grace to follow You, the Way, to learn from You, the Truth, and live in You, the Life.[277] Jesus, You are lover of my soul, hide me, O my Saviour, hide me till the storm of life is past, safe into the haven guide. I have placed all my trust in You. Cover my defenseless head with the shadow of Your wing; I cast my care to Your gracious hand![278] Thank you, Lord Jesus, that You will be my hiding place whatever happens.[279] Lord Jesus, make Yourself to me a living, bright reality. More present to faith's vision keen than any outward object seen.[280]

---

[274] Jeremy Taylor, 1613-67

[275] Psalm 64:10 (Amplified Bible)

[276] Psalm 65:2-3 (Amplified Bible)

[277] Desiderius Erasmus

[278] Charles Wesley

[279] Corrie ten Boom

[280] Hudson Taylor

I believe in You: God, the Father almighty, Creator of heaven and earth. I believe in Jesus Christ, Your only son, my Lord. He was conceived by the power of the Holy Spirit and born of the Virgin Mary. He suffered under Pontius Pilate, was crucified, died, and was buried. He descended to the dead. On the third day he rose again. He ascended into heaven, and is seated at the right hand of the Father. He will come again to judge the living and the dead. I believe in the Holy Spirit, the holy catholic Church, the communion of saints, the forgiveness of sins, the resurrection of the body, and the life everlasting. Amen.[281]

Lord, I believe with joy all that is contained in the creeds of the apostles. I trust my heart to You: One God in three persons, Father, Son, and Holy Spirit.

I come and see the works of God. I see how to save Your people You dealt with their foes. I see how you have provided for Your people. You turned the sea into dry land, they crossed through the river on foot; there they rejoiced in You. I, too, join in rejoicing in Your works.[282] GOD be merciful and gracious me and bless me and cause Your face to shine upon me and amongst us! -- That Your way may be known upon earth, Your saving power, Your deliverances and Your salvation among all nations.[283]

I am enfolded in the Father, and I am enfolded in the Son, and I am enfolded in the Holy Spirit. And the Father is enfolded in me, and the Son is enfolded in me, and the Holy Spirit is enfolded in me: almightiness, all wisdom, all goodness: one God, one Lord.[284] Holy Father, keep me in Your truth; Holy Son, protect me under the wings of Your cross; Holy Spirit,

---

[281] The Apostles' Creed
[282] Psalm 66:5-6 (Amplified Bible)
[283] Psalm 67:1-2 (Amplified Bible)
[284] Julian of Norwich

make me a temple and dwelling place for Your glory; grant me Your peace all the days of my live, O Lord.[285]

I bind to myself the name, the strong name of the Trinity; by invocation of the same, The Three in One, and One in Three. Of whom all nature has creation; eternal Father, Spirit, Word: Praise to the Lord of my salvation, salvation is of Christ the Lord.[286]

May I wake after a good night's sleep with renewed energy to do Your will and be faithful to the heavenly vision and the sacred call You have placed on my life. I love You Lord.

---

[285] Office of Compline, Maronite Church

[286] St Patrick

Reading: Psalm 68 ☐ ☐

Let Us Pray . . .

May Christ's words be in my mind, on my lips and in my heart.[287] Enable me, O God, to collect and compose my thoughts before an immediate approach to You in prayer. May I be careful to have my mind in order when I take upon myself the honour to speak to the Sovereign Lord of the universe, remembering that upon the temper of my soul depends, in very great measure, my success. You are infinitely too great to be trifled with, too wise to be imposed on by a mock devotion, and abhor a sacrifice without a heart. Help me to entertain an habitual sense of your perfections, as an admirable help against cold and formal performances. Save me from engaging in rash and precipitate prayers and from abrupt breaking away to follow business or pleasure as though I had never prayed.[288]

O Lord, my heavenly Father, almighty and everlasting God, who brought me safely to the beginning of this day: Defend me with Your mighty power; and grant that this day I fall into no sin, neither run into any kind of danger; but that I, being ordered by Your governance, may do always what is righteous in Your sight; through Jesus Christ our Lord. In confidence of your goodness and great mercy, O Lord, I draw near to You, as a sick person to the Healer, as one hungry and thirsty to the Fountain of life, a creature to the Creator, a desolate soul to my own tender Comforter. Behold, in You is everything that I can or ought to desire. You are my salvation and my redemption, my helper and my strength.[289]

Give me a candle of the Spirit, O God, as I go down

---

[287] Phrase used at the Proclamation of the Gospel – with small sign of the cross

[288] Susanna Wesley, 1669-1742

[289] Thomas a Kempis

into the depths of my being. Show me the hidden things, the creatures of my dreams, the storehouse of forgotten memories and hurts. Take me down to the spring of my life, and tell me my nature and my name. Give me freedom to grow, so that I may become that self, the seed of which You planted in me at my making. Out of the deep I cry to you, O God.[290]

Write Your blessed name, O Lord, upon my heart, there to remain so indelibly engraved, that no prosperity, no adversity will ever move me from Your love. Be to me a strong tower of defence, a comforter in tribulation, a deliverer in distress, a very present help in trouble and a guide to heaven through the many temptations and dangers of this life.[291] My God, I put myself without reserve into Your hands. What have I in heaven, and apart from You what do I want upon earth? My flesh and my heart fail, but God is the God of my heart, and my portion forever.[292]

Blessed be the Lord, who bears my burdens and carries me day by day, even the God who is my salvation! Lord God, You are the God of deliverances and salvation. You have made a way for me to escape from death and You have set me free. O God, awe-inspiring, profoundly impressive, and great You are. You give strength and fullness of might to Your people. I am among those blessed. Blessed be God![293] Compassionate Healer, remove the heart of stone in me and give me a heart of flesh. Grace my life with the fullness of the Spirit within me.[294] Lord help me today to find new, fresh ways of letting the world know that because You are alive in my heart, there is a celebration is going on. Amen.

---

[290] Jim Cotter (based on a prayer by George Appleton)

[291] Thomas a Kempis

[292] J.H. Newman

[293] Psalm 68:19, 20, 35 (Amplified Bible)

[294] Ezekiel 36

Reading: Psalms 69 ☐ ☐ 70 ☐ ☐

Let Us Pray . . .

My God and my all.[295] Holy, holy, holy, the Lord God the Almighty, who was and is and is to come.[296] Your presence, Jesus, makes this created world joyous and free. Eternal God be the portion of my soul; let heaven be my inheritance and hope; let Christ be my Head, and my promise of security; let faith be my wisdom, and love my very heart and will, and patient persevering obedience be my life; and then I can spare the wisdom of the world, because I can spare the trifles that it seeks, and all that they are like to get by it.[297]

Fill my life, O Lord my God, in every part with praise, that my whole being may proclaim Your being and Your ways. Not for the lip of praise alone, nor the praising heart I ask, but for a life made up of praise in every part![298] Be my vision, O Lord of my heart; naught be all else to me, save that You art, You be my best thought, by day or by night, waking or sleeping, Your presence my light.[299]

Eternal God, the light of minds who know You, the life of the souls who love You, the strength of the wills who serve You; help me so to know You that I may truly love You, so to love You that I may fully serve You, whom to serve is perfect freedom.[300]

The Lord says: *Love the Lord your God with your whole heart.* Today, did I: Keep You in mind and put You first in my life? or was I too caught up in material concerns? Did I

---

[295] Francis of Assisi, 1181-1226

[296] Revelation 4:8

[297] Richard Baxter

[298] Horatius Bonar

[299] Traditional Irish

[300] Gelasian Sacramentary, based on a prayer by Augustine

worship You, my God, reverently and meaningfully, wherever I was? Did I respect Your holy name, or have I dishonored You by using Your name in anger and carelessness? Did I pray to You even when I don't feel like it and habituate a constant awakeness to Your presence? Did I seriously and joyfully trust You as my God and live as one attuned to Your personal love and concern for me? Did I genuinely repent of my sins and accept Your free and gracious forgiveness?

But I am poor and needy; come to me, O God! You are my Help and my Deliverer![301] Save me, O God, for the waters have come up to my neck and threaten my life. I sink in deep mud, where there is no foothold; I have come into deep waters, where the floods overwhelm me. Rescue me out of the mud, and let me not sink; let me be delivered from those who hate me and from out of the deep waters.[302] I will praise Your name O God with a song and will magnify You with thanksgiving.[303]

All-knowing and ever-loving God, help me to see people, not through the glasses of my impoverished humanity and my own woundedness, but as You see them.[304] I need Your transformation in my life.[305]

O God, King of Righteousness, lead me in the ways of justice and of peace; inspire me to break down all tyranny and oppression, to gain for every person due reward and from every person due service; that each may live for all, and all may care for each, in the name of Jesus Christ.[306]

---

[301] Psalm 70:5 (Amplified Bible)

[302] Psalm 69:1, 2, 14 (Amplified Bible)

[303] Psalm 69:30 (Amplified Bible)

[304] Jean Vanier, Encountering the Other, p. 19

[305] Romans 12:1-4

[306] William Temple, 1881-1944

Reading: Psalm 71 ☐ ☐

Let Us Pray . . .

Our father, who is in heaven hallowed be Your name. Let Your kingdom come. Your will be fulfilled, as well in earth, as it is in heaven. Give me this day my daily bread. And forgive me my trespasses, even as I forgive those who trespass me. Lead me not into temptation: but deliver me from evil, for Yours is the kingdom and the power, and the glory for ever. Amen.[307] You are holy, Lord, the only God and Your deeds are wonderful. You are strong, You are great. You are the most high, You are almighty. You, holy Father, are King of heaven and earth. You are three and one, Lord God, all good. You are good, all good, supreme good, Lord God, living and true. You are Love, You are Wisdom You are Humility, You are Endurance. You are Rest, You are Peace. You are Joy and Gladness, You are Justice and Moderation. You are all riches, and You suffice for us. You are Beauty, You are Gentleness. You are my Protector, You are my Guardian and Defender. You are Courage, You are my Haven and my Hope. You are my Faith, my Great Consolation. You are my Eternal Life, great and wonderful Lord. God Almighty, Merciful Saviour.[308]

I will hope continually, and I will praise You more and more with each succeeding day. My mouth will tell of Your righteous acts and of Your deeds of salvation, for their number is more than I know. I will come in the strength and with the mighty acts of the Lord God; I will mention and praise Your righteousness, for You alone are the Holy God.[309] O heavenly Father, in whom I live and move and have my being: I humbly pray for

---

[307] Matthew 6:9-13 (Tyndale New Testament Version)

[308] Francis of Assisi, 1181-1226

[309] Psalm 71:14-16 (Amplified Bible)

You to so guide and govern me by Your Holy Spirit, that in all the cares and occupations of my life I do not forget You, but remember that I am ever walking in Your sight; through Jesus Christ our Lord. Amen.

Most high, most great and good Lord, to You belong praises, glory and every blessing; to You alone do they belong, most high. May You be blessed, my Lord, for the gift of all Your creatures and especially for our brother sun, by whom the day is enlightened. He is radiant and bright, of great splendour, bearing witness to You, O my God. May You be blessed, my Lord, for our sister the moon and the stars; You have created them in the heavens, fair and clear. May you be blessed, my Lord, for my brother the wind, for the air, for cloud and calm, for every kind of weather, for through them You sustain all creatures. May You be blessed, my Lord, for our sister water, which is very useful, humble, pure and precious. May You be blessed, my Lord, for our brother fire, bright, noble and beautiful, untamable and strong, by whom You illumine the night. May You be blessed, my Lord, for our mother the earth, who sustains and nourishes us, who brings forth all kinds of fruit, herbs and brightly coloured flowers. May You be blessed, my Lord, for those who pardon out of love for You, and who patiently bear illness and tribulation. Happy are those who abide in peace, for through You, most high God, they will be crowned. May You be blessed, my Lord, for our sister death of body, from whom no living person can escape. Woe to the person who dies in a state of mortal sin. Happy are those who at the hour of death are found in obedience to Your holy will, for the second death cannot hurt them. Praise and bless, my Lord; give Him thanks and serve Him with great humility.[310]

---

[310] Francis of Assisi, 'Canticle of the Sun'

**Reading: Psalms 72 ☐ ☐
73 ☐ ☐**

Let Us Pray . . .

Blessed be the Lord God, the God of Israel, Who alone does wondrous things! Blessed be Your glorious name forever; let the whole earth be filled with Your glory! Amen and Amen![311] Whom have I in heaven but You, O Lord? And I have no delight or desire on earth besides You. My flesh and my heart may fail, but You my God are the rock and firm strength of my heart and my portion forever. It is good for me to draw near to You; I have put my trust in You as my Lord and God and made You my refuge, that I may tell of all Your works.[312]

O happy day, that fixed my choice on You, my Saviour and my God! Well may this loving heart rejoice, and tell its raptures all abroad. O happy bond, that seals my vows to You who merits all my love! Let cheerful anthems fill Your house, while to that sacred shrine I move. It's done: the great transaction's done! I am the Yours and You are mine; You drew me to Yourself and I followed on; charmed to confess the voice divine. Happy day, happy day, when You Jesus washed my sins away! You taught me how to watch and pray, and live rejoicing every day Happy day, happy day, when Jesus washed my sins away.[313] Let all the world in every corner sing, *My God and King!* The heavens are not too high, Your praises there may grow, the church with psalms must shout, no door can keep them out. Let all the world in every corner sing, `My God and King!'[314]

The Lord says: *Love one another as I have loved you.* Be quick, O God, to expose my

---

[311] Psalm 72:18-19 (Amplified Bible)
[312] Psalm 73:25-28 (Amplified Bible)

[313] Philip Doddridge
[314] George Herbert

little efforts, pitiful fakery and lame excuses designed to avoid Your life-giving work of love in and through me. Today, have I loved my parents and brothers and sisters and tried to create a happy home life? Or am I sometimes thoughtless, hurtful or indifferent toward those I love? Have I been fair and honest in my relationships? Or do I sometimes fake it or take unfair advantage of others by cheating, stealing, or lying? Have I contributed to the welfare and flourishing of my workplace, school or home? Or do I ridicule and gossip without trying to make things better? Have I respected the rights and sensitivities of others? Or am I prejudiced at times, perhaps with unconscious biases, and do I tend to put people in categories or ignore them because they are different? Have I honestly forgiven people who dislike me? Or have I tried to hurt them by what I've said or done? Have I been grateful for my sexuality and grown in sexual maturity and responsibility? Or do I sometimes exploit members of the opposite sex or entertain unwholesome thoughts? Have I tried to improve the quality of life around me? Or do I foul up the environment and waste the good things I have stewardship for? Have I cared about my country and the good of the human community? Or do I care only about myself and the people I know? Have I been concerned for the poor, the hungry, those in prison, the vulnerable, the destitute and for the millions who thirst for justice and peace? Have I found ways to contribute to the poor of the world?

Lord, forgive me the hatreds, prejudices and malice which pull the rug from under all my so-called love for others and for you. So many peoples feed on hatred for one another, endlessly suppressing the truth of our common humanity. Save me from this, I pray.

Our Father who is in the heavens! hallowed be Your name. 'Your reign come: Your will come to pass, as in heaven also on the earth. 'My appointed bread give me to-day. And forgive me my debts, as also I have forgiven my debtors. 'And lead me not to temptation, but deliver me from the evil, because Yours is the reign, and the power, and the glory -- to the ages. Amen.[315]

My Defender, I leave my own protection in Your hands, give to me love for my enemies. When I awake tomorrow, may I resolve to do good to those who hate me, speak evil of me and who design to bring harm to me. Lord, give courage and compassion, a liberation of the spirit, an opening of heart and mind, so that those thought of only as aliens and enemies may become simply people. I prayer through the Friend of sinners, Jesus Christ the one who became vulnerable for my sake.[316]

In this hour of this day, fill me, O Lord, with Your mercy, that rejoicing throughout the whole day, I may take delight in Your praise, through Jesus Christ our Lord.[317]

---

[315] Matthew 6:9-13 (Young's Literal Translation)

[316] Christopher Avon Lamb

[317] Sarum Missal

Reading: Psalms 74 ☐ ☐ 75 ☐ ☐

Let Us Pray . . .

Prone to wonder, Lord I feel it. Prone to leave the God I love. Here's my heart, Lord, take and seal it. Seal it for Your courts above. O Immanence, who knows nor far nor near, but as the air I breathe is with me here, my breath of life, O Lord, I worship You.[318] Almighty and everlasting God, by whose Spirit the whole body of Your faithful people is governed and sanctified: Receive my supplications and prayers so I may truly serve You, through my Lord and Saviour Jesus Christ. I give praise and thanks to You, O God, I praise and give thanks. Your wondrous works declare that Your name is near and those who invoke Your name rehearse Your wonders.[319] You are my King, working salvation in the midst of the earth. The day is Yours, the night also is Yours. You have established the starry skies and the sun. You have fixed all the borders of the earth, the divisions of land and sea and established the nations. You have made summer and winter.[320]

Amazing grace! how sweet the sound that saved a wretch like me; I once was lost, but now am found; was blind, but now I see. 'Twas grace that taught my heart to fear, and grace my fear relieved; how precious did that grace appear, the hour I first believed! Through many dangers, toils and snares I have already come: 'Tis grace that brought me safe thus far, and grace will lead me home. Lord, You have promised good to me, Your Word my hope secures; You will my shield and portion be as long as life endures. Yes, when this heart and flesh shall fail, and mortal life shall cease, I shall profess within the veil a life of joy and peace. When I've been there a thousand years, bright shining as the sun, I've no less days to sing

---

[318] Amy Carmichael, 1868-1951
[319] Psalm 75:1 (Amplified Bible)
[320] Psalm 74:12, 16, 17 (Amplified Bible)

Your praise than when I first began.[321]

Lord, may I be no person's enemy, and may I be the friend of that which is eternal and abides. May I never quarrel with those nearest me: and if I do, may I be reconciled quickly. May I love, seek, and attain only that which is good. May I wish for all happiness and envy none. May I never rejoice in the ill-fortune of one who has wronged me. When I have done or said what is wrong, may I never wait for the rebuke of others, but always rebuke myself until I make amends. May I win no victory that harms either me or my opponent. May I reconcile friends who are angry with one another. May I, to the extent of my power, give all needful help to my friends and all who are in want. May I never fail a friend who is in danger. When visiting those in grief may I be able by gentle and healing words to soften their pain. May I respect myself. May I always keep tame that which rages within me. May I accustom myself to be gentle, and never be angry with people because of circumstances. Through Jesus Christ who came in the flesh, lived a perfect life and in perfect death shed His blood for me.[322]

Lord, make me to walk in Your way: Where there is love and wisdom, there is neither fear nor ignorance; where there is patience and humility, there is neither anger nor annoyance; where there is poverty and joy, there is neither greed nor avarice; where there is peace and contemplation, there is neither care nor restlessness; where there is the fear of God to guard the dwelling, there no enemy can enter; where there is mercy and prudence, there is neither excess nor harshness; this I know through Your Son, Jesus Christ our Lord.[323]

---

[321] John Newton

[322] Eusebius, 3rd century

[323] Francis of Assisi, 1182-1226

Reading: Psalms 76 ☐ ☐ 77 ☐ ☐ 78:1-31 ☐ ☐

Let Us Pray . . .

Let my mouth be filled with Your praise, O Lord, that I may sing of Your glory, for You have counted me worthy to partake of Your holy divine, immortal and life-giving mysteries: preserve me in Your holiness, that I may learn of Your righteousness all the day long. Alleluia, Alleluia, Alleluia.[324] Today I give to You what I can not keep; to gain that which I cannot lose.[325]

You Lord are to be feared, with awe and reverence! Who may stand in Your presence when once Your anger is roused?[326] I will meditate upon all Your works and consider all Your mighty deeds. Your way, O God, is in holiness, away from sin and guilt. Who is a great God like our God? You are the God Who does wonders; You have demonstrated Your power among the peoples.[327] Spirit of the Living God, help me in my weaknesses to pray as I ought to and where I have no words, Spirit intercede with sighs too deep for words. Search my heart and intercede, according to the will of my God.[328]

O God and Lord of the Powers, and Maker of all creation, who, because of Your clemency and incomparable mercy, sent Your only begotten Son and our Lord Jesus Christ for the salvation of humankind, and with His venerable cross He tore asunder the record of my sins, and thereby conquered the rulers and powers of darkness; receive from sinful me, O merciful Master, these prayers of gratitude and supplication, and deliver me from every destructive and gloomy transgression, and from all visible and invisible enemies who seek to injure me. Nail down my flesh with reverence of

---

[324] Liturgy of John Chrysostom and Basil the Great
[325] Jim Elliott
[326] Psalm 76:7 (Amplified Bible)
[327] Psalm 77:12-14 (Amplified Bible)
[328] Romans 8:26-28

You, and let not my heart be inclined to words or thoughts of evil, but pierce my soul with Your love, that ever contemplating You, being enlightened by You, and discerning You, the unapproachable and everlasting Light, I may unceasingly render confession and gratitude to You: The eternal Father, with Your Only-Begotten Son, and with Your All-Holy, Gracious, and Life-Giving Spirit, now and ever, and unto ages of ages. Amen.[329]

Jesus You said: *Be perfect as your heavenly Father is perfect.* So today I ask, have I worked at becoming a better person and a better Christian? Have I made the most of my talents, my education and my opportunities? Or do I fail to use these sometimes? Have I placed wisdom and the application of knowledge above reputation, or grades? Have I taken care of my body, and made sure I am getting enough sleep and exercise? Have I eaten and consumed too much or misused or abused my body with alcohol or other drugs? Have I been able to admit my own need for help and to ask for it? Have I accepted myself, despite my limitations and weakness? Have I sorted out my fundamental orientation to life and aligned with my God-given purpose?

Eternal God You are my strength, in my darkness my light, in my sorrow my comfort and peace. May I always live in Your presence, and serve You in my day to day life; through Jesus Christ my Lord.[330]

To You, Creator of nature and humanity, of truth and beauty, I pray: Hear my voice, for it is the voice of the victims of all wars and violence among persons and nations. Hear my voice, for it is the voice of all children who suffer and will suffer when people put their faith in weapons and war. Hear my voice when I beg You to

---

[329] Basil the Great

[330] Boniface

instill into the hearts of all human beings the wisdom of peace, the strength of justice and the joy of fellowship. Hear my voice, for I speak for the multitudes in every country and in every period of history who do not want war and are ready to walk the road of peace. Hear my voice and grant insight and strength so that those with whom I live and work and I, too, may always respond to hatred with love, to injustice with total dedication to justice, to need with the sharing of self, to war with peace. O God, hear my voice, and grant unto the world Your everlasting peace.[331]

---

[331] (Pope) John Paul II

Reading:
Psalm 78:32-end ☐ ☐

Let Us Pray . . .

Almighty Lord God, Your glory cannot be approached, Your compassion knows no bounds, and Your love for all humankind is beyond human expression. In Your mercy look on me and all Your people: do not leave us to our sins but deal with me and us according to Your goodness. Guide me to the haven of Your will and make me truly obedient to Your commandments, that I am not ashamed when I come before your Messiah's dread judgment seat. For You, O God, are good and ever-loving, and I glorify You Father, Son and Holy Spirit, now and forever, to the ages of ages.[332]

I remember that You O God are my Rock, and the Most High God, my Redeemer.

You are full of mercy and compassion, You forgave my iniquity and didn't destroyed me. Many times You have turned Your anger away and did not stir up Your wrath and indignation, though I was deserving of it.[333]

Our Father who is in heaven, hallowed be Your name. Your kingdom come. Your will be done on earth as it is in heaven. Give me this day my daily bread. And forgive me my debts, as I forgive my debtors. And lead me not into temptation, but deliver me from evil. For Yours is the kingdom, and the power, and the glory, for ever. Amen.[334]

I weave into my life this day the presence of You, my God - upon my way, in this hour, I weave into my life Your mighty power. I weave into my sore distress Your peace and calm and no less. I weave into my step so lame,

---

[332] Orthodox Liturgy

[333] Psalm 78:35, 38 (Amplified Bible)

[334] Matthew 6:9-13 (Webster's Bible Translation)

healing and helping of Your name. I weave into the darkest night strands of Your shining bright. I weave into each deed done joy and hope of the Risen Son. I weave tonight Your presence bright. I weave tonight the sacred Light. Lord I realize that love doesn't mean doing extraordinary or heroic things. I means knowing how to do ordinary things with tenderness.[335] Help me to realize this in my actions throughout this day. I will bless the Lord at all times; His praise shall continually be in my mouth.[336] My spirit is dry within me because it forgets to feed on You.[337] You are holy, Lord, the only God, and Your deeds are wonderful. You are strong. You are great. You are the most high. You are almighty holy Father; You are King of heaven and earth. You are three and one, Lord God, all Good. You are my eternal life, great and wonderful Lord, God almighty, merciful Saviour.[338]

O be joyful in the Lord my soul; serve the Lord with gladness. I come now before Your presence with a song. I know that You Lord are God; it is You who has made me and not me myself; it is true that I am one of Your chosen people and a sheep of Your pasture. I go on my way through Your gates with thanksgiving and into Your courts with praise; I am thankful to You and search to speak good of Your Name. For You Lord are gracious; Your mercy is everlasting; and Your truth endures from generation to generation.[339]

Breathe into me, Holy Spirit, that my mind may turn to what is holy. Move me, Holy Spirit, that I may do what is holy. Stir me, Holy Spirit, that I may love what is holy. Strengthen me, Holy Spirit, that I may preserve what is holy. Protect me, Holy Spirit, that I may never lose what is holy.[340]

---

[335] Jean Vanier

[336] Psalm 34:1 NRSV

[337] John of the Cross

[338] Francis of Assisi

[339] Traditional Jubilate Psalm 100

[340] Saint Augustine

Reading: Psalms 79 ☐ ☐ 80 ☐ ☐

Let Us Pray . . .

What can I say to You, my God? Will I collect together all the words that praise Your holy name? Shall I give You all the names of this world, You, the Unname-able? Shall I call you God of my life, meaning of my existence, my journey's end, home of my loneliness and aloneness? Shall I say: Creator, Sustainer, Pardoner, Near One, Distant One, Incomprehensible One, God of the gentle wind and of terrible battles, Wisdom, Power, Loyalty, and Truthfulness, Eternity and Infinity, You the All-merciful You the just One, You are love itself?[341] Reveal, O Lord, to my eyes Your glory. Expose, O Lord, to my heart Your love. Disperse, O Lord, from my mind the darkness. Fill, O Lord, my life with Your light. Protect, O Lord, from thoughts without action. Guard, O Lord, from words without feelings. Defend, O Lord, from ideas without results. And surround me with Your presence. Open my eye, my heart, my mind, my will, and my soul to the infilling of Your Spirit.

Grant to me, Lord, joy in giving, joy in receiving. Love incoming, love outflowing. Peace instilling, peace distilling. Wisdom infilling, wisdom outpouring. Grant to me, Lord, a rhythm of life. Help me, O God of my salvation, for the glory of Your name! Deliver me, forgive me, and purge away my sins for Your name's sake.[342] Restore me, O Lord God of hosts; cause Your face to shine in pleasure, approval, and favour on me, and I will be saved![343]

I give thanks to You Lord, for You are good; Your steadfast love endures for ever! I was pushed hard, so

---

[341] Karl Rahner

[342] Psalm 79:9 (Amplified Bible)

[343] Psalm 80:19 (Amplified Bible)

that I was falling, but You helped me ... You are my God, and I will give thanks to You; You are my God, I will extol You.[344]

From jealousy, whether of equals or superiors, from begrudging others' successes, from impatience of submission and eagerness for authority: Give me the spirit of common fellowship to share with fellow-workers in all true proportion; and from all insubordination to just laws and proper authority: Save and help me, O LORD.

From all hasty utterances of impatience, from the retort of irritation and the taunt of sarcasm, from all infirmity of temper in provoking or being provoked; and from all idle words that may do hurt: Save and help me, O LORD.

O God, Giver of Life, Bearer of Pain, Maker of Love, You are able to accept in me what I cannot even acknowledge: You are able to name in me what I cannot bear to speak of You are able to hold in Your memory what I have tried to forget; You are able to hold out to me the glory that I cannot conceive of. Reconcile me through Your cross to all that I have rejected in myself, that I may find no part of Your creation to be alien or strange to me, and that I may be made whole, through Jesus Christ, my lover and my friend.[345]

God be with my going out,
God be with my coming in,
God be with me in my doubt,
God protecting me from sin.
Christ be with my ebbing,
Christ be with my flowing,
Christ be with my entering,
Christ in love bestowing.
Spirit with me every hour,
Spirit at the journey's end,
Spirit be my every power,
Spirit dove on me descend.

---

[344] Psalm 118:1, 13, 28 NRSV

[345] Janet Morley

Reading: Psalms 81 ☐ ☐ 82 ☐ ☐

Let Us Pray . . .

Arise, O God, judge the earth! For to You belong all the nations.[346] I sing aloud to God my Strength! I shout for joy to the God of Jacob![347] O Lord my God, most merciful, most secret, most present, most constant, yet changing all things, never new and never old, ever in action yet ever quiet, creating, upholding, and perfecting all, who has anything but Your gift? Or what can any person say when they speak to You? Yet have mercy upon me, O Lord, that I might speak to You and praise Your name.[348]

Be the strength between me and each weakness. Be the light between me and each darkness. Be the joy between me and each sadness. Be the calm between me and each madness. Be the life of God between me and each death. Be the Spirit of God between me and each breath. Be the love of God between me and each sigh. Be the Presence of God with me when I die.

Our Father who is in the heavens, let Your name be sanctified, let Your kingdom come, let Your will be done as in heaven so upon the earth; give me today my needed bread, and forgive me my debts, as I also forgive my debtors, and lead me not into temptation, but save me from evil.[349]

I confess that the world I see seems stronger than the world unseen and the world of "uncertainty" and "sense" much stronger than the world of faith, trust and risk. The needs of the world are daunting, overwhelming and almost impossible to fathom, much less resolve. Help me

---

[346] Psalm 82.8 (Amplified Bible)
[347] Psalm 81:1 (Amplified Bible)
[348] Jeremy Taylor, 1613-67 (based on Augustine)

[349] Matthew 6:9-13 (Darby Bible Translation)

to know that life for me and others is better when I live with expectation and hope rather than pessimism, cynicism, gloom and disillusionment. I want to be mindful of dual realities and I need Your help to navigate life and living on earth O Lord.[350]

O Lord God, destroy and root out whatever the adversary plants in me, that with my sins destroyed You may sow understanding and good work in my mouth and heart; so that in act and in truth I may serve only You and know how to fulfill the commandments of Christ and to seek Yourself. Give me love, give me self-discipline, give me faith, give me all things which You know belong to the profit of my soul. O Lord, work good in me, and provide me with what you know that I need.[351]

In all times of temptation to follow pleasure, to leave duty for amusement, to indulge in distraction, dissipation, dishonesty, or debt, or to degrade my high calling and forget my solemn vows; And in all times of frailty in my flesh: Save and help me, O LORD.[352]

Lord Jesus Christ, You stretched out Your arms of love on the hard wood of the cross that everyone might come within the reach of Your saving embrace: So clothe me in Your Spirit that I, reaching forth my hands in love, may, by the power of Your Spirit, be instrumental in bringing those who do not know You to the knowledge and love of You; for the honour of Your name. Amen.

Gracious God, hear my prayers and, in Your love, answer. Yours is the Kingdom, the power and the glory, now and forever. Amen.

---

[350] Adapted from Ernerson's Prayers for the People

[351] Columbanus, c. 550-615

[352] From Southwell Litany

Reading: Psalms 83 ☐ ☐ 84 ☐ ☐ 85 ☐ ☐ 86 ☐ ☐

Let Us Pray . . .

Holy, holy, holy is the Lord God Almighty, who was, who is, and who is to come.[353] O Lord my God, You are above all things - the best, the strongest and most high. You alone most full and most sufficient, You alone the sweetest, full of consolation. You alone most noble and glorious beyond all things, for in You are gathered all good things. Never may my heart find rest unless it rests with You.[354] How lovely are the places where You reside, O Lord of hosts! My soul yearns, yes, even pines and is homesick for the courts of the Lord; my heart and my flesh cry out and sing for joy to the living God. O Lord God of hosts, hear my prayer; give ear, O God of Jacob! For a day in Your courts is better than a thousand anywhere else. Your presence is my joy.[355]

Awaken me, Lord to Your light, open my eyes to Your presence. Awaken me, Lord to Your love, open my heart to Your indwelling. Awaken me, Lord to Your life, open my mind to Your abiding. Awaken me, Lord to Your purpose, open my will to Your guiding.

Father, bless to me the dawn, bless to me the coming morn. Bless all that my eyes will see. Bless all that will come to me. Bless my neighbour and my friend. Bless the stranger at my door. Bless all who to me are dear. Bless, O Lord, this day of days. Bless and grace me in Your all knowing ways.

Will You not revive me again, that I may rejoice in You? Show me Your mercy and loving-kindness, O Lord, and grant me Your salvation. I will listen with expectancy to

---

[353] Revelation 4.8

[354] Thomas a Kempis, c.7380-1471

[355] Psalm 84:1, 2, 8, 10a (Amplified Bible)

what You, as Lord over all, will say, for You will speak peace to Your people, to those who are in right standing with You. Let me not turn again to my self confident folly. Keep me safe from myself, O LORD.[356]

Give ear, O Lord, to my prayer; and listen to the cry of my supplications. Teach me Your way, O Lord, that I may walk and live in Your truth; direct and unite my heart to reverently honor Your name. I will confess and praise You, O Lord my God, with my whole heart; and I will glorify Your name forevermore.[357] Please do not keep silent, O God; don't hold Your peace or be still, O God, I pray.[358]

In all times of ignorance and perplexity as to what is right and best to do; direct me with wisdom to judge aright, and order my ways, and overrule my circumstances by Your good Providence, and in all my mistakes and misunderstandings: Save and help me, O LORD.

From strife, partisanship, and division, from magnifying my certainties to condemn all differences, from building systems to exclude all challenges and include only preferred people, and from all arrogance in my dealings with others: Save and help me, O LORD..

Give me a knowledge of myself: my power and weaknesses, my spirit, my sympathy, and my imagination, my knowledge, my truth. Teach me by the standard of your Word, by the judgments of others, by examination of myself. Give me an earnest desire to strengthen myself continually by study, diligence, prayer, and meditation. And from all fancies, delusions, and prejudices of habit, or temper, or society: Save and help me, O LORD.[359] Lord, in Your mercy, hear my prayer.

---

[356] Psalm 85:6-8 (Amplified Bible)

[357] Psalm 86:6, 11, 12 (Amplified Bible)

[358] Psalm 83.1 (Amplified Bible)

[359] From Southwell Litany

Reading: Psalms 87 ☐ ☐ 88 ☐ ☐

Let Us Pray . . .

I praise You for the life that stirs within me: I praise You for the bright and beautiful world into which I go. I praise You for earth and sea and sky, for cloud and singing bird. I praise You for the work You have given me to do. I praise You for all that You have given me to fill my leisure hours. I praise You for my friends: I praise You for music and books and good company and all pure pleasures.[360] Thanks be to the Father Who gives me light and guides my way. Thanks be to the Saviour Who gives me love and hears me pray. Thanks be to the Spirit Who gives me life and is with me to stay. The earth is Your dwelling, live in me Lord, let me live in you. Settle in my heart, please be at home in my will, at rest in my mind, at ease in my strength, that I might reside in peace, live in joy, abide in love, and inhabit eternity.

O LORD, the God of my salvation, I have cried to You for help by day, at night I am in Your presence. Let my prayer come before You and really enter into Your presence; incline Your ear to my cry. But to You I cry, O Lord, and in the morning shall my prayer come to meet You.[361]

Lord you are in this place, fill me with Your power, cover me with Your peace, show me Your presence. Lord help me to know that I am in Your hands, under Your protection, and covered by Your love. Lord I ask You today to deliver me from evil, to guide me in my travels, and to defend me from all harm. Lord give me now, eyes to see the invisible, ears to hear Your call, hands to do Your work, and a heart to respond to Your love. What is before me today, I don't

---

[360] John Baillie, 1886-1960

[361] Psalm 88:1, 2, 13 (Amplified Bible)

know, whether I will live or die; but this I do know, that all things are ordered and sure. Everything is ordered with unerring wisdom and unbounded love, by You, my God, You are love. Grant me in all things to see Your hand, through Jesus Christ my Lord.[362]

Our Father in heaven, may Your name be kept holy. Let Your kingdom come. Let Your pleasure be done, as in heaven, so on earth. Give me this day bread for my needs. And make me free of my debts, as I have made those free who are in debt to me. And let me not be put to the test, but keep me safe from the Evil One.[363]

O Lord, show Your mercy to me and grant me Your salvation. Make way for Your chosen people to be joyful. Give peace, O Lord, in all the world, for only in You can I flourish and live in safety. O God, I thank You for all the joy I have had in life.[364] God, You work in me increasingly, and You give me my appointed tasks for this day. Help me to steadfastly fulfill the duties of my calling. When I am called to account, may I be found faithful and enter into Your eternal joy.[365]

In the name of Jesus Christ, who lives and reigns with You and the Spirit, one God, now and forever. Amen

---

[362] Charles Simeon, 1759-1836

[363] Matthew 6:9-13 (Bible in Basic English)

[364] Byrhtnoth, 10th century

[365] Anglican prayer

Reading: Psalm 89 ☐ ☐

Let Us Pray . . .

Glory to God for all things![366] I will sing of the mercy and loving-kindness of the Lord forever. With my mouth will I make known Your faithfulness from generation to generation. For mercy and loving-kindness shall be built up forever; Your faithfulness will You establish in the very heavens. Blessed are the people who know the joyful sound and who understand and appreciate the spiritual blessings afforded by Your grace. They walk, O Lord, in the light and favour of Your countenance! In Your name they rejoice all the day, and in Your righteousness they are exalted.[367] That this evening may be holy, good and peaceful: I pray to You, O Lord. That Your holy angels will lead me in the paths of peace and goodwill: I pray to You, O Lord. That I may be pardoned and forgiven for my sins and offences: I pray to You, O Lord. That there may be peace in Your Church and for the whole world: I pray to You, O Lord. That I may be bound together with others by Your Holy Spirit, in communion all Your saints, entrusting one another and all my life to Christ: I pray to you, O Lord.[368]

Give me true knowledge of others, in their difference from me and in their likeness to me, that I may deal with their real selves not merely measuring their feelings by my own, but patiently considering their varied lives and thoughts and circumstances. And in all my dealings with them, from false judgments of my own, from misplaced trust and distrust, from misplaced giving and refusing, from misplaced praise and blame: Save and help me, O LORD.

---

[366] John Chrysostom, c.347-407
[367] Psalm 89:1, 2, 15, 16 (Amplified Bible)
[368] Source unknown (Orthodox Litany)

Chiefly, I pray that I may know You and see You in all Your works, always feel Your presence near, hear You and know Your call. Let Your Spirit be my will, Your Word, my word. And in all my shortcomings and infirmities, may I have sure faith in Your mercy: Save and help me, O LORD.

Finally, I pray, blot out my past transgressions, heal the evils of my past negligences and ignorances, and help me to amend my past mistakes and misunderstandings. Uplift my heart to new love, new energy, new devotion, that I may be unburdened from the grief and shame of past unfaithfulness and go forth in Your strength to persevere, through success and failure, through good report and evil report, even to the end. And in all time of my tribulation and in all time of my prosperity: Save and help me, O LORD.[369]

Before I go to rest, I commit myself to Your care through Christ, and call upon You to forgive me for all my sins of this day past, and I ask that You would keep alive Your grace in my heart, and that You would cleanse me from all sin, pride, harshness, and selfishness, and give me, instead, the spirit of meekness, humility, firmness, and love. O Lord, keep Yourself present to me ever, and perfect Your strength in my weakness. Take me under Your blessed care, this night and evermore; through Jesus Christ our Lord.[370]

O Lord, cleanse my mind, I call upon You, of all anxious thoughts for myself, that I may learn not to trust in the abundance of what I have, other than as tokens of Your goodness and grace, but that I may commit myself in faith to Your keeping, and devote all my energy of soul, mind and body to the work of Your kingdom and the furthering of the purposes of Your divine righteousness, through Jesus Christ our Lord.[371]

---

[369] From Southwell Litany

[370] Thomas Arnold, 1795-1842

[371] Euchologium Anglicanum

Reading: Psalms 90 ☐ ☐ 91 ☐ ☐ 92 ☐ ☐

Let Us Pray . . .

Glory to God in the highest, and peace to all people on this earth.

It is a good and delightful thing to give thanks to the Lord, to sing praises to Your name, O Most High, to show forth Your loving-kindness in the morning and Your faithfulness by night, For You, O Lord, have made me glad by Your works; at the deeds of Your hands I joyfully sing. How great are Your doings, O Lord! Your thoughts are very deep.[372] He who dwells in the secret place of the Most High shall remain stable and fixed under the shadow of the Almighty, whose power no foe can withstand. I will say of the Lord, He is my Refuge and my Fortress, my God; on Him I lean and rely, and in Him I confidently trust![373]

Most high and glorious God, enlighten the darkness of my heart and give me a true faith, a certain hope and a perfect love. Give me a sense of the divine and knowledge of Yourself, so that I may do everything in fulfilment of Your holy will, through Jesus Christ our Lord.[374]

O Lord my God, thank You for bringing this day to a close; thank You for giving me rest in body and soul. Your hand has been over me and has guarded and preserved me. Forgive my lack of faith and any wrong that I have done today, and help me to forgive all who have wronged me. Let me sleep in peace under Your protection, and keep me from all the temptations of darkness. Into Your hands I commend my loved ones and all who dwell in this place. I commend to You my body

---

[372] Psalm 92:1, 2, 4, 5 (Amplified Bible)

[373] Psalm 91:1-2 (Amplified Bible)

[374] Francis of Assisi, 1182-1226

and soul. O God, Your holy name be praised.[375]

Lord, my heavenly Father, You order all things for our eternal good, mercifully enlighten my mind, and give me a firm and abiding trust in Your love and care. Silence my murmurings, quiet my fears, and dispel my doubts, that rising above my afflictions and my anxieties, I may rest on You, the rock of everlasting strength.[376]

Lord, keep this and all nations under Your care; and guide me and us in the way of justice and truth. Let Your way be known upon earth; Your saving health among all nations. O Lord, let not the needy be forgotten; nor the hope of the poor be taken away.

Into Your hands, most blessed Jesus, I commend my soul and body, for You have redeemed both by Your most precious blood. So bless and sanctify my sleep to me, that it may be temperate, holy, and safe, a refreshment to my weary body, to enable it so to serve my soul, that both may serve You with never-failing duty. Visit me with Your grace and favour. Teach me to number my days, that I may apply my heart to wisdom, and ever be mindful of my last end.[377] So teach me to number my days, that I may receive a heart of wisdom. O satisfy me with Your mercy and loving-kindness in the morning now, before I get much older, that I might rejoice and be glad all the days You have given. And let the beauty, delightfulness and favour of my Lord God be upon me; confirm and establish the work of my hands.[378]

When the day returns, call me with a morning face, and with morning heart, eager to labour, happy if happiness be my portion, and if the day is marked for sorrow, strong to endure.[379] As Jesus taught us

---

[375] Dietrich Bonhoeffer
[376] New Church Book of Worship, 1876
[377] Jeremy Taylor, 1613-67
[378] Psalm 90:12, 14, 17 (Amplified Bible)
[379] Robert Louis Stevenson, 1850-94 (written and read to his family on the eve of his unanticipated death)

to pray: Our Father who is in heaven, hallowed be Your name. Your kingdom come, Your will be done in earth, as it is in heaven. Give me this day my daily bread. And forgive me my debts, as I forgive my debtors. And lead me not into temptation, but deliver me from evil: For Yours is the kingdom, and the power, and the glory, forever. Amen.[380]

Give me a sense of humour Lord; together with some things to laugh about today. Give me the grace to take a joke against me and to see the funny side of the things I do and say. Shield me from sourness, annoyance, being annoying, bad tempered, moody, and resentful towards others. Lighten my seriousness and fill my heart with the joy and love of Jesus.

I sing to You a new song, for You have done marvelous things; Your right hand and Your holy arm have brought salvation. You, Lord, have made known Your salvation; Your righteousness has been openly shown to the nations.[381]

Into Your hands, O Lord, I commend myself this day. Let Your presence be with me til its close. Strengthen me to remember that in whatsoever good work I do I am serving You. Give me a diligent and watchful spirit, that I may seek in all things to know Your will, and knowing it, gladly to perform it; to the honour of Your name.[382]

Glory to God in the highest, and peace to all people on this earth.

---

[380] Matthew 6:9-13 (American King James Version)

[381] Psalm 98:1-2 (Amplified Bible)

[382] Source unknown

Reading: Psalms 93 ☐ ☐ 94 ☐ ☐ 95 ☐ ☐

Let Us Pray . . .

LORD You reign, You are clothed with majesty. You have girded Yourself with strength and power; the world also is established, that it cannot be moved. Your throne is established from of old; You are from everlasting.[383] I come and sing to the Lord; I make a joyful noise to the Rock of my salvation! I come before Your presence with thanksgiving; I make a joyful noise to You with songs of praise! I have come to worship and bow down, to kneel before You, the Lord my Maker. For You are my God and I am a person of Your pasture and a sheep of Your hand. Today, I hear Your voice and obey.[384] O Father, I will trust You: for all the known and all the unknown good that I have ever had has come from You. Sweet Saviour, I will trust You. Your grace is all-sufficient for my soul, as mighty as Your power and as matchless as Your love. Blest Spirit, I will trust You: how can I ever dare to trust myself, to think, or speak, or act apart from You? O God, my God, my hope and stay, who knows and orders all that is best, I know not what to will or do aright; then make me ever love to choose and do Your will.[385]

Lord, You know the thoughts of each person, that they are vain, empty and futile-only a breath. Blessed am I because You love me, You discipline and instruct me. O Lord teach me out of Your Word. When I said, my foot is slipping, Your mercy and loving-kindness hold me up. In the multitude of my anxious thoughts within me, Your comforts cheer and delight my soul! You Lord are my High Tower, my Defense, and my God, the Rock of my refuge.[386] Stay with me, Lord: the day is

---

[383] Psalm 93:1-2 (Amplified Bible)
[384] Psalm 95:1, 2, 6, 7 (Amplified Bible)
[385] Walter Howard Frere, 1863-1938
[386] Psalm 94:11, 12, 18, 19, 22 (Amplified Bible)

almost over and it is getting dark.[387]

Lord, I pray this day mindful of the sorry confusion of this world. Look with mercy upon this generation of Your children so steeped in misery of their own contriving, so far strayed from Your ways and so blinded by passions. I pray for the victims of tyranny, that they may resist oppression with courage. I pray for wicked and cruel men and women, whose arrogance reveals what the sin of my own heart is like when it has conceived and brought forth its final fruit. I pray for myself and those I love that as we live in peace and quietness, that we may not regard our good fortune as proof of our virtue, or rest content to have our ease at the price of other people's sorrow and tribulation. I pray for all who have some vision of Your will, despite the confusions and betrayals of human sin, that they may humbly and resolutely plan for and fashion the foundations of a just peace between peoples, even while they seek to preserve what is fair and just among us against the threat of malignant powers.[388]

O sweet and loving God, when I stay asleep too long, oblivious to all Your many blessings, then, please, wake me up, and sing to me Your joyful song. It is a song without noise or notes. It is a song of love beyond words, of faith beyond the power of human telling. I can hear it in my soul, when You awaken me to Your presence.[389]

My God, I thank You for loving me. I am sorry for all my sins, for not loving others and for not loving You as I ought. Help me to live like Jesus lived, and not sin again.

---

[387] Luke 24.29 (Good News Bible)

[388] Reinhold Niebuhr, 1892-1971

[389] Mechthild of Magdeburg, c.1210-c.1280

Reading: Psalms 97 ☐ ☐
98 ☐ ☐ **99** ☐ ☐ **100** ☐ ☐

Let Us Pray . . .

I extol the Lord my God and worship at Your footstool! Holy are You O God! I extol You Lord, my God, and worship at Your holy hill, for the Lord is holy![390] Take, Lord, and receive all my liberty, my memory, my understanding, and all my will, all that I have and possess. You have given them to me; to You, O Lord, I restore them; all things are Yours, dispose of them according to Your will. Give me Your love and Your grace, for this is enough for me.[391]

O Lord, I do not pray for tasks equal to my strength: I ask for strength equal to my tasks.[392] O God, your Word tells me that, whatever my hand finds to do, I must do it with my might. Help me today to concentrate with my whole attention on whatever I am doing, and keep my thoughts from wandering and my mind from straying. When I am studying, help me to study with my whole mind. When I am playing, help me to play with my whole heart. Help me to do one thing at a time, and to do it well. This I ask for Jesus' sake.[393]

O Lord, prepare me for all the events of the day, for I don't know what the day may bring. Give me grace to deny myself, to take up my cross today, and to follow in the steps of my Lord and Master.[394] Help me to remember, O God, that every day is Your gift, and ought to be used according to Your command, through Jesus Christ our Lord.[395] Lord, be with me this day, within me to purify me, above me to draw me up, beneath me to sustain me, before me to lead me, behind me to restrain me, around me to protect

---

[390] Psalm 99:5, 9 (Amplified Bible)
[391] Ignatius Loyola, 1491-1556
[392] Phillips Brooks, 1835-93
[393] William Barclay
[394] Matthew Henry, 1662-1714
[395] Samuel Johnson, 1709-84

me.[396] God give me work till my life's end, and life till my work is done.[397] As has been prayed: Lord, You know how busy I must be this day. If I forget You, I pray You will not forget me.[398]

Lord, whatever this day may bring, Your name be praised.[399] O be joyful in the Lord my soul. I seek to serve the Lord with gladness and come before Your presence with a song. I know that You Lord are God; it is You who has made me and not me myself. It is true that I am one of Your chosen people and a sheep of Your pasture. I go on my way through Your gates with thanksgiving and into Your courts with praise. I am thankful to You and search to speak good of Your Name. For You Lord are gracious, Your mercy is everlasting; and Your truth endures from generation to generation.[400]

Our Father who is in heaven, Hallowed be Your name. Your kingdom come, Your will be done in earth, as it is in heaven. Give me this day my daily bread. And forgive me my debts, as I forgive my debtors. And lead me not into temptation, but deliver me from evil. For Yours is the kingdom, and the power, and the glory, forever. Amen.[401]

You LORD reign, let the earth rejoice; let the multitude of isles and coastlands be glad! Light is sown for the uncompromising righteous, and there is joy for the upright in heart, an irrepressible joy which comes from consciousness of Your favour and protection.[402]

---

[396] Saint Patrick, c.389-c.461

[397] Source unknown (Found on the grave of Winifred Holtby, 1898-1935)

[398] Jacob Astley, 1579-1652 (Prayed before commanding troops at the battle of Edgehill, 23 October 1642, first battle of English Civil War)

[399] Dietrich Bonhoeffer (Written while awaiting execution in a Nazi prison)

[400] Traditional Jubilate Psalm 100

[401] Matthew 6:9-13 (Geneva Study Bible)

[402] Psalm 97:1, 11 (Amplified Bible)

**Reading: Psalms 101 ☐
☐ 102 ☐ ☐ 103 ☐ ☐**

Let Us Pray . . .

As I rejoice in the gift of this new day, so may the light of Your presence, O God, set my heart on fire with love for You; now and forever.[403] Fill me, I pray, with Your light and life, that I may show Your wondrous glory. Grant that Your love may so fill my life that I count nothing too small to do for You, nothing too much to give and nothing too hard to bear.[404]

At the beginning You existed and laid the foundations of the earth, the heavens are the work of Your hands. But You remain the same, and Your years will have no end. The children of Your servants will dwell safely and continue, and their descendants will be established before You.[405] For as the heavens are high above the earth, so great are Your mercies and loving-kindness toward those who reverently and worshipfully fear You. As far as the east is from the west, so far have You removed my transgressions from me. As a father loves and pities his children, so You love and pity those of us who fear You and come to You in reverence, worship, and awe.[406] O Lord my God, You have chased the slumber from my eyes, and once more brought me to a place where I can lift up my hands to You and praise Your just judgements, accept my prayers and supplications, and give me faith and love. Bless my coming in and my going out, my thoughts, words, and works, and let me begin this day with the praise of the unspeakable sweetness of Your mercy. Hallowed be Your name. Your kingdom come, through Jesus Christ our Lord.[407]

That this evening may be holy, good, and peaceful, I pray, O Lord. That Your holy

---

[403] The Daily Office
[404] Ignatius Loyola, 1491-1556
[405] Psalm 102:25, 27, 28 (Amplified Bible)
[406] Psalm 103:11-13 (Amplified Bible)
[407] Greek Liturgy, 3rd century

angels will lead me in paths of peace and goodwill, I pray, O Lord. That I may be pardoned and forgiven for my sins and offenses, I pray, O Lord. That there may be peace in Your Church and in the whole world, I pray, O Lord. That I might be bound together with other believers by Your Holy Spirit, and that we increasingly entrust one another and all our lives to Christ, I pray, O Lord.

Almighty God, You have so linked my life with others so that all I do affects, for good or ill, other lives: so guide me in the work I do, that I may do it not for myself alone, but for the common good. And, as I seek a proper return for my own labour, make me mindful of the rightful aspirations of other workers, and arouse my concern for those who are out of work, through Jesus Christ, who lives and reigns with You and the Holy Spirit, one God, for ever and ever.[408]

O Lord: In a world where many are lonely, I thank You for my friendships. In a world where many are captive, I thank You for my freedom. In a world where many are hungry, I thank You for Your provision. I pray that You will: enlarge my sympathy, deepen my compassion, and give me a grateful heart. In Christ's name.[409] I will sing of Your mercy and loving-kindness and justice. To You, O Lord, will I sing. I will behave myself wisely and give heed to the blameless way, O when will You come to me? I will walk within my house in integrity and with a blameless heart. I will set no wicked thing before my eyes. I hate the work of those who turn aside from the right path.[410] Praise to the Creator, praise to the Son, praise to the Spirit, the Three in One.

---

[408] Source unknown

[409] Terry Waite

[410] Psalm 101:1-3a (Amplified Bible)

Reading: Psalm 104 ☐ ☐

Let Us Pray . . .

Lord, this morning I give You worship with all my life, obedience with all my power, praise with all my strength, honour with all my speech, love with all my heart, affection with all my sense, my being with all my mind, and I give you my soul. O Most High and Holy God.[411]

Our Father who is in Heaven, may Your name be kept holy. Let Your kingdom come, let Your will be done, as in Heaven so on earth. Give me and those I love today our bread for the day; and forgive us our shortcomings, as we also have forgiven those who have failed in their duty towards us. And bring us not into temptation, but rescue each of us from the Evil one.[412]

This new day You give to me from Your great eternity. This new day now enfolds me in Your loving hold. You are the star of the morn, You are the day newly born, You are the light of my night, You are the Saviour by Your might. God be in me this day. God ever with me stay. God be in the night, keep me by Your light. God be in my heart. God abide, never depart.[413] Teach me, O God not to torture myself, not to make a martyr of myself through stifling reflection; but rather teach me to breathe deeply in faith, through Jesus, our Lord.[414]

O Lord my God, as You have in mercy preserved me to the beginning of another day, enable me, by Your grace, to live as unto You and to set my affections and attentions on things above, not on things upon the earth. Pour into my mind the light of Your truth and cause me to rejoice in Your word. Shed abroad Your love in my heart, and graciously give to me the peace and comfort of

---

[411] Adapted from Alexander Carmichael (1900)

[412] Matthew 6:9-13 (Weymouth New Testament Version)

[413] David Adam

[414] Soren Kierkegaard, 1813-55

Your Holy Spirit, for the sake of Jesus Christ my Lord.[415]

Father; I abandon myself into Your hands, do with me what You will. Whatever You may do, I thank You; I am ready for all, I accept all. Let only Your will be done in me - I wish no more than this, O Lord. Into Your hands I commend my soul; I offer myself to You with all the love of my heart, for I love You Lord, and so need to give myself, to surrender myself into Your hands, without reserve, and with boundless confidence, for You are my loving Father.[416] O Lord, keep me this day without sin. O Lord, have mercy upon me and have mercy upon all of us. O Lord, let Your mercy be upon me; as my trust is in You. O Lord, in You have I trusted; let me never be confounded.

Create in me a clean heart, O God; and sustain me with Your Holy Spirit. O Lord, save Your people, and bless Your heritage. Govern me and lift me up forever. Day by day I magnify You; and I worship Your name forever, world without end.

I bless and gratefully praise You Lord! O Lord my God, You are very great! You are clothed with honor and majesty-- O Lord, how many and varied are Your works! In wisdom have You made them all; the earth is full of Your riches and Your creatures. May Your glory endure forever; may I continually join you in rejoicing in Your works--I will sing to You Lord as long as I live; I will sing praise to You, my God, while I have any being. 34May my meditation be sweet to You; O my soul, I will rejoice in the Lord.[417]

---

[415] Isaac Ashe, 19th century

[416] Jesus Caritas

[417] Psalm 104:1, 24, 31, 33, 34 (Amplified Bible)

Reading: Psalm 105 ☐ ☐

Let Us Pray . . .

Lord God, whose Son, my Saviour Jesus Christ triumphed over the powers of death and prepared for me my place in the new Jerusalem, grant that I, having given thanks for Your resurrection, may praise You in that place of which Jesus Christ is the Light, and where He lives and reigns, for ever and ever.

I believe in God, the Father Almighty, Creator of heaven and earth. I believe in Jesus Christ, His only Son, our Lord. He was conceived by the power of the Holy Spirit and born of the Virgin Mary. He suffered under Pontius Pilate, was crucified, died, and was buried. He descended to the dead. On the third day He rose again. He ascended into heaven, and is seated at the right hand of the Father. He will come again to judge the living and the dead. I believe in the Holy Spirit, the holy catholic Church, the communion of saints, the forgiveness of sins, the resurrection of the body, and the life everlasting. Amen.[418]

O Triune God, the source of eternal light: Shed forth Your unending day upon me as I watch for You, that my lips may always praise You, that my life, well lived, may bless You, and my worship tonight and tomorrow might give You worthy glory, through Jesus Christ my Lord. Amen.

Most holy God, the source of all good desires, all right judgments, and all just works: Give to me, as Your servant, that peace which the world cannot give, so that my mind may be fixed on the doing of Your will, and that I, delivered from the fear of all enemies, may live in peace and quietness; through the mercies of Christ Jesus my Saviour.

I give thanks to You Lord, I call upon Your name, please make known Your doings among the peoples! I sing

---

[418] The Apostles' Creed

praises to You; I meditate on and talk of all Your marvelous deeds and devoutly praise them. I glory in Your holy name; let the hearts of those of us who see You as indispensable to our lives rejoice. I seek and crave You. I need to know and experience Your strength, Your might and inflexibility to temptation; I seek Your face and to continually in Your presence. I earnestly remember the marvelous deeds that You have done, Your miracles and wonders, the judgments and sentences which You pronounced upon Your enemies.[419]

O God, my Father, help me through this day to live in a way that brings help to others, credits the name I bear, and bring joy to those who love me, and to You. May I be cheerful when things go wrong; persevering when things are difficult; serene when things are irritating. Enable me to be helpful to those in difficulties, kind to those in need, sympathetic to those whose hearts are sorrowful and sad. Grant that nothing may make me lose my temper, nothing may take away my joy, nothing may ruffle my peace, nothing may make me bitter towards anyone. So, grant that through all this day all those with whom I work, and all those whom I meet, may see in me the reflection of the Master, whose I am, and whom I seek to serve. This I ask for Your love's sake.[420] Lord, You know what I want, if it be Your will that I have it, and if it be not Your will, good Lord, do not be displeased, for I want nothing which You do not want.[421]

Faithful Creator God, whose mercy never fails, as I sleep and as tomorrow unfolds, deepen my faithfulness to You for Your only Son, Jesus Christ's sake. Amen

---

[419] Psalm 105:1-5 (Amplified Bible)

[420] William Barclay

[421] Julian of Norwich, 1342-c.1416

Reading: Psalm 106 ☐ ☐

Let Us Pray . . .

O God, make speed to save me. O Lord, make haste to help me. Your face, Lord, I seek this morning. Lord turn Your face towards me and shine Your face upon me and those I love, and those with whom I have to do – today.[422] Guard and protect my family today O LORD. Grant that putting You first in all my loving, I might be liberated from all lesser loves and loyalties, and have You as my First Love, my Chief Good, and my Final Joy.[423]

O Jesus, fill me with Your love. I call upon You, accept me, and use me a little for Your glory. I earnestly call upon You to accept me and my service as it is given in Christ's name, and take all the glory for Yourself.[424] May my life be a gift to Your honour and glory. Come, Lord Jesus![425] Lord God almighty, open my heart and enlighten by the grace of Your Holy Spirit, that I may seek what is well-pleasing to Your will; direct my thoughts and affections to think and to do such things as may make me worthy to attain to the unending joys in heaven; and so order my doings after Your commandments that I may be ever diligent to fulfil them, and be found to be worthy in Christ for everlasting reward.[426] All through this day, O Lord, may I touch as many lives as You would have me touch for You, whether by the word I speak, the letter I write, the prayer I breathe, or the life I live.[427]

O God, You make me glad with the remembrance of the glorious resurrection of Your Son, my Lord. Grant me this day such blessing through my worship of You, that the days to come may be spent in Your favour; through Jesus Christ my Lord. Give me, Lord, a stout heart to bear

---

[422] Psalm 27:8
[423] Adapted from George Appleton
[424] David Livingstone, 1813-73
[425] Revelation 22.20
[426] Bede, 675-735
[427] Source unknown

my own burdens, a tender heart to bear the burdens of others, and a believing heart to lay all my burdens on You, for You care for me and You care for us.[428]

I praise the Lord! Hallelujah! O give thanks to the Lord, for He is good, for His mercy and loving-kindness endure forever! Who can put into words and tell the mighty deeds of the Lord? Or who can show forth all the praise that is due You? Blessed are those who observe justice by treating others fairly and who do right and are in right standing with God at all times. Deliver me, O Lord my God, and pull me towards Yourself that I may give thanks to Your holy name and glory in praising You. Blessed be the Lord, the God of Israel, from everlasting to everlasting! And let all the people say, Amen! Praise the Lord! Hallelujah![429]

I arise today through a mighty strength: Your power to guide me. Your might to uphold me. Your eyes to watch over me. Your word to give me speech. Your hand to guard me. Your way to lie before me; Your shield to shelter me. Your host to secure me. Thanks be to my God.[430] Show me Your mercy, O Lord, and grant me Your salvation. Clothe all Your ministers and international workers with righteousness; let Your people sing with joy. Give peace, O Lord, in all the world; for only in You can we live in safety. Lord, keep this nation under Your care; and guide me in the way of justice and truth. Let Your ways be known upon earth; Your saving health among all nations. Let not the needy be forgotten, O Lord; nor let the hope of the poor be taken away. Create in me a clean heart, O God; and sustain me by Your Holy Spirit.

---

[428] Lesslie Newbigin

[429] Psalm 106:1-3, 47, 48 (Amplified Bible)

[430] Adapted from Saint Bridgid of Gael (5th Century)

Reading: Psalm 107 ☐ ☐

Let Us Pray . . .

I praise You, O God. I acclaim You as the Lord over all. All creation joins me in worship of You, the Father Everlasting. To You all angels, all the powers of heaven, the cherubim and seraphim, say in endless praise: Holy, Holy, Holy Lord, God of power and might, heaven and earth are full of Your glory.[431]

Use me, then, my Saviour, for whatever purpose, and in whatever way, You may require. Here is my poor heart, an empty vessel, fill it with Your grace. Here is my sinful and troubled soul, quicken it and refresh it with Your love. Take my heart for Your home, my mouth to spread abroad the glory of Your name, my love and all my powers, for the advancement of your believing people; and never suffer the steadfastness and confidence of my faith to abate; so that at all times I may be enabled from the heart to say, Jesus needs me, and I am His.[432]

You say to me: *Love the Lord your God with your whole heart.* Before You, I ask: Do I keep You in mind and put You first in my life? or am I too caught up in material concerns? Do I worship You regularly and carefully? Do I respect Your name or have I dishonoured You in any way? Do I pray even when I don't feel like it? Do I trust You and live in the light and warmth of Your personal love and concern for me? Do I genuinely repent of my sins and accept Your gracious forgiveness? Fix my steps, O Lord, so that I don't stagger at the uneven motions of the world, but steadily go towards my glorious home. The winds are often rough, and my own weight presses me downwards. Reach forth, O Lord, Your hand, Your saving hand, and speedily deliver me. Lord, let me not live to be useless.[433]

---

[431] From *Te Deum Laudamus*

[432] Dwight L. Moody, 1837-99

[433] John Wesley, 1703-91

Lord, without You I can do nothing; with You I can do all. Help me by Your grace, that I don't fall; help me by Your strength, to resist mightily the very first beginnings of evil, before it takes hold of me. Help me to cast myself at once at Your sacred feet, and lie still there, until the storm is past. And, if I lose sight of You, bring me back quickly to You, and grant that I love You better, for Your tender mercy's sake.[434]

Write Your blessed name, O Lord, upon my heart, there to remain so indelibly engraved, that no prosperity, no adversity shall ever move me from Your love. Be to me a strong tower of defence, a comforter in tribulation, a deliverer in distress, a very present help in trouble, and a guide to heaven through the many temptations and dangers of this life.[435]

O give thanks to the Lord, for You are good; for Your mercy and loving-kindness endure forever! Let the redeemed of the Lord say so, You have delivered me from the hand of the adversary, Oh, that humankind would praise You Lord for Your goodness and loving-kindness and Your wonderful works! ⁹For You satisfy my longing soul and fill the hungry of my soul with good.[436]

May You, God, make me steadfast in faith, joyful in hope and untiring in love all the day and nights of my life.[437] Be, Lord Jesus, a bright flame before me, a smooth path below me: Today, tonight, forever. Amen.[438]

---

[434] Edward Bouverie Pusey, 1800-82

[435] Thomas a Kempis, c.1380-1471

[436] Psalm 107:1, 2, 8, 9 (Amplified Bible)

[437] Adapted from Roman liturgy

[438] Saint Columba (6th Century)

Reading: Psalms
108 ☐ ☐ 109 ☐ ☐

Let Us Pray . . .

Jesus, grant me grace to fix my mind on You, especially in times of prayer, when I commune directly with You. Stop the motions of my wandering head, and the desires of my unstable heart; suppress the power of my spiritual enemies, who try to draw me away.[439]

Dear Jesus, help me to spread your fragrance everywhere I go today. Flood my soul with Your spirit and life. Penetrate and possess my whole being so utterly that my life may only be a radiance of Yours. Shine through me, and be so in me, that every person I come in contact with may feel Your presence in their inner person. Let them look up and see no longer me but only Jesus! Stay with me, and then I will begin to shine as You shine Lord. I want to share the Light with others; the light, O Jesus, will be all from You, none of it will be mine; it will be You, shining on others through me. Let me preach You without preaching, not by words but by my God-energized example, by the catching force, the sympathetic influence of what I do, the evident fullness of the love my heart bears to You.[440]

O good Shepherd, seek me out, and bring me home to Your fold again. Deal favourably with me according to Your good pleasure, till I dwell in Your house all the days of my life, and praise You forever.[441] Deal with me and act for me, O God the Lord, for Your name's sake, because Your mercy and loving-kindness are good, O deliver me. For I am poor and needy, and my heart is wounded and stricken within me. Help me, O Lord my God; O save me according to Your mercy and loving-kindness![442] Almighty God, whose most dear Son first

---

[439] Adapted from Richard Whitford

[440] Cardinal Newman, 1801-90 (Prayed daily by Mother Teresa's Missionaries of Charity)

[441] Jerome, c.342-420

[442] Psalm 109:21, 22, 26 (Amplified Bible)

suffered pain and anguish before He was crucified: Mercifully grant that I, walking in the way of the cross, may find it none other than the way of life and peace, through Your Son Jesus Christ our Lord. Father, give to me, and to all Your people: in times of anxiety, serenity, in times of hardship, courage, in times of uncertainty, patience, and, at all time, a quiet trust in Your wisdom and love, through Jesus Christ my Lord.[443]

O GOD, my heart is fixed with the confidence of faith given me. I will sing, yes, I will sing praises, even with all the faculties and powers of one created by You, in Your image! I will wake early--I will waken the dawn! I will praise and give thanks to You, O Lord, among the peoples, and I will sing praises to You among the nations. Have You not cast me off, O God? And will You not go forth, O God, with our armies? Give me help against the adversary, for vain is the help of humankind. Through and with God I shall do valiantly, for You shall tread down my adversaries.[444]

Oh blessed Lord! How much I need Your light to guide me on my way! So many hands, that, without heed, still touch Your wounds and make them bleed, so many feet that day by day still wander from Your fold astray! Feeble at best is my endeavour! I see but cannot reach the height that lies forever in the Light; and yet forever and forever, when seeming just within my grasp, I feel my feeble hands unclasp, and sink discouraged into night, for Your own purpose You have sent the strife and the discouragement.[445]

---

[443] New Every Morning

[444] Psalm 108:1-3, 12, 13 (Amplified Bible)

[445] Henry Wadsworth Longfellow, 1807-82

Reading: Psalms
110 ☐ ☐   111 ☐ ☐

Let Us Pray . . .

Let the words of my mouth and the meditations of my heart be acceptable in Your sight, O Lord, my strength and my redeemer.[446]

O my God, I believe in You, I hope in You, and I love You, because You have created me and those I love; You redeemed me, and sanctify me. Increase my faith, strengthen my hope, and deepen my love, that giving up myself wholly to Your will, I may serve You faithfully all the rest of my life, through Jesus Christ our Lord.[447] I bind myself to You today O Trinity.

Pilgrim God, there is an exodus going on in my life: the desert stretches, a vast land of questions. Inside my head Your promises tumble and turn. No pillar of cloud by day or fire by night that I can see. My heart hurts at leaving loved ones and so much of the security I have known. I try to give in to the stretching and the pain. It is hard, God, and I want to be settled, secure, safe and sure. And here I am feeling so full of pilgrim's fear and anxiety. O God of the journey, lift me up, press me against Your cheek. Let Your great love hold me and create a deep trust in me. Then set me down, God of the journey; take my hand in Yours, and guide me ever so gently across the new territory of my life.[448]

O Lord, my Lord, who has decided that all human beings, whatever their colour or race, are equal before You: break down the hatred between peoples, especially hatred due to national and ethnic differences. I ask You to help those in whose hands are the various governments, parties, tribes and clans of the world. Reconcile them to one another, so that each may respect the rights of the other. I ask all this in the

---

[446] Psalm 19:14

[447] The Narrow Way, 1869

[448] Joyce Rupp

name of my Saviour, Jesus Christ.[449]

Have mercy on me, O God, according to Your unfailing love, according to Your great compassion blot out my transgressions. Wash away all my iniquity and cleanse me from my sin. For I know my transgressions, and my sin is always before me. Against You, You only, have I sinned and done what is evil in Your sight. So You are right in Your verdict and justified when You judge. Surely I was sinful at birth, sinful from the time my mother conceived me. Yet You desired faithfulness even in the womb. You taught me wisdom in that secret place. Cleanse me with hyssop, and I will be clean, wash me, and I will be whiter than snow. Let me hear joy and gladness, let the bones You have crushed rejoice. Hide Your face from my sins and blot out all my iniquity. Create in me a pure heart, O God, and renew a steadfast spirit within me. Do not cast me from Your presence or take Your Holy Spirit from me. Restore to me the joy of Your salvation and grant me a willing spirit, to sustain me. Then I will teach transgressors Your ways, so that sinners will turn back to You. Deliver me from the guilt of bloodshed, O God, You who are God my Saviour, and my tongue will sing of Your righteousness. Open my lips, Lord, and my mouth will declare Your praise. You do not delight in sacrifice, or I would bring it; You do not take pleasure in burnt offerings. My sacrifice, O God, is a broken spirit, a broken and contrite heart You, God, will not despise.[450]

Lord, give my body restful sleep, and let the work I have done today be sown for an eternal harvest, through Christ our Lord. Again I say, let the words of my mouth and the meditations of my heart be acceptable in Your sight, O Lord, my Strength and my Redeemer.[451]

---

[449] Student Christian Movement (Zambia)

[450] Psalm 51

[451] Psalm 19:14

Reading: Psalms

112 ☐ ☐   113 ☐ ☐

114 ☐ ☐

Let Us Pray . . .

I praise the Lord! Hallelujah! Praise the name of the Lord! Blessed be the name of the Lord from this time forth and forever. From the rising of the sun to the going down of it and from east to west, the name of the Lord is to be praised![452]

Praise the Lord! Hallelujah! I delight greatly in Your commandments. Your offspring will be mighty upon earth, the generation of the upright shall be blessed. Light arises in the darkness for the upright, gracious, compassionate, and just who are in right standing with God.[453]

Almighty God, who after the creation of the world rested from all Your works and sanctified a day of rest for all Your creatures: Grant that I might put away all earthly anxieties, may be duly prepared for Your service on earth, and that Your willingness to be my Sabbath on earth may be a preparation for the eternal rest promised to Your people in heaven, through Jesus Christ our Lord. Amen.

Dear Lord, help me keep my eyes on You. You are the incarnation of divine love, You are the expression of God's infinite compassion, You are the visible manifestation of the Father's holiness. You are beauty, goodness, gentleness, forgiveness, and mercy. In You all can be found. Outside of You nothing can be found. Why should I look elsewhere or go elsewhere? You have the words of eternal life, You are food and drink, You are the Way, the Truth, and the Life. You are the light that shines in the darkness, the lamp on the lampstand, the house on the hilltop. You are the perfect icon of God. In and through You I can see and find my way to the Heavenly Father.

---

[452] Psalm 113:1-3 (Amplified Bible)

[453] Psalm 112:1, 2, 4 (Amplified Bible)

O Holy One, Beautiful One, Glorious One, be my Lord, my Saviour, my Redeemer, my Guide, my Consoler, my Comforter, my Hope, my joy, and my Peace. To you I want to give all that I am. Let me be generous, not stingy or hesitant. Let me give You all-all I have, think, do, and feel. It is Yours, O Lord. Please accept it and make it fully Your own.[454]

Lord my God, great, eternal, wonderful in glory, You who keeps covenant and promises with those who love You with their whole heart, You who are the Life of all, the Help of those who flee to You, the Hope of those who cry to You, cleanse me from my sins, secret and open. And from every thought displeasing to Your goodness, cleanse my body and soul, my heart and conscience, that with a pure heart, and a clean soul, with perfect love and calm hope, I may venture confidently and fearlessly to pray to You, through Jesus Christ my Lord.[455]

Lord of compassion, You love me. You call to me as a mother calls to her child. But the more You call to me, the more I turned away. Yet You were the one who taught me to walk. You took me up in Your arms. But I did not acknowledge that You took care of me. You drew me to Yourself. You picked me up, and held me to Your cheek. You bent down to me and fed me. Lord of Compassion, do not give me up, do not abandon me. Do not punish me in Your anger![456] Tremble, O earth, at the presence of the Lord, at the presence of the God of Jacob, Who turned the rock into a pool of water, the flint into a fountain of waters.[457]

From Your hand O God, I receive everything. I place everything into Your hand, O Saviour, entrust everything.

---

[454] Henri Nouwen

[455] Coptic Liturgy of St Basil

[456] Philip Law (based on Hosea 11.1-9)

[457] Psalm 114:7-8 (Amplified Bible)

Let us make our way together, Lord. Wherever You go I must go and through whatever You pass, there too I will pass.[458]

For my deceitful heart and crooked thoughts. For barbed words spoken deliberately. For thoughtless words spoken hastily. For envious and prying eyes. For ears that rejoice in iniquity and rejoice not in the truth. For greedy hands. For wandering and loitering feet: For haughty looks, have mercy upon me, O God.[459]

Today Almighty God, give me wisdom to perceive You, intellect to understand You, diligence to seek You, patience to wait for You, eyes to behold You, a heart to meditate upon You and life to proclaim You, through the power of the Spirit of our Lord Jesus Christ.[460]

---

[458] Teresa of Avila, 1515-82

[459] John Baillie, 1886-1960

[460] Benedict, 480-543

Reading: Psalms
115 ☐ ☐ 116 ☐ ☐ 117 ☐ ☐

Let Us Pray . . .

Eternal Light, shine into my heart this evening. Eternal Goodness, deliver me from evil. Lord God, You are Life, Wisdom, Truth, Beauty, and Blessedness, the Eternal, the True Good. My God and my Lord, You are my hope and my heart's joy. Eternal Power, be my support. Eternal Wisdom, scatter the darkness of my ignorance. Eternal Pity, have mercy upon me; that with all my heart, mind, soul and strength I might seek Your face and be brought by Your infinite mercy into Your holy presence, through Jesus Christ my Lord.[461]

I love You, O my God; and I desire to love You more and more. Grant to me that I may love You as much as I desire, and as much as I ought. O dearest friend, who has so loved and sought to save all of us, the thought of whom is so sweet and always growing sweeter, come with Christ and dwell in my heart; then You will keep a watch over my lips, my steps, my deeds, and I will not need to be anxious either for my soul or my body. Give me love, sweetest of all gifts, which knows no enemy. Give me in my heart pure love, born of Your love to me, that I may love others as You love me. O most loving Father of Jesus Christ, from whom flows all love, let my heart, frozen in sin, cold to You and cold to others, be warmed by this divine fire. So help and bless me in Your Son.[462] O Lamb of God, who takes away the sins of the world, grant me Your peace.[463]

Be my light in the darkness, O Lord, and in your great mercy defend me from all

---

[461] Alcuin of York (804)

[462] Anselm, 1033-1109

[463] Church of England *Book of Common Prayer*

perils and dangers of this night; for the love of your only Son, our Saviour Jesus Christ. Bring me safety through to the morning hours, through Him who died and rose again for me, Your Son my Saviour Jesus Christ. Lord Jesus, stay with me for the evening is at hand and the day is past. Be my companion in the way, rekindle my heart, and awaken warranted hope, that, as on the road to Emmaus, I might know You as You are revealed in Scripture and the breaking of bread. Grant this for the sake of Your love. Amen

I love You Lord, because You heard and now hear my voice and my supplications. Because You have inclined Your ear to me, therefore will I call upon You as long as I live. Return to rest, O my soul, for the Lord has dealt bountifully with you. For You have delivered my life from death, my eyes from tears, and my feet from stumbling and falling. I will walk before the Lord in the land of the living.[464]

O praise the Lord, all you nations! Praise Him, all you people! For His mercy and loving-kindness are great toward us, and the truth and faithfulness of the Lord endure forever. Praise the Lord! Hallelujah![465] Not to me, O Lord, not to me but to Your name give glory, for Your mercy and loving-kindness and for the sake of Your truth and faithfulness![466]

I go to sleep with Your blessing. One day my last evening will come when I enter eternity. Let me now so live that all that I do in time maybe a preparation for that last blessed place, so that vision may follow faith, possession succeed hope, perfect union replace imperfect love, for You are my final End and greatest Good.[467]

---

[464] Psalm 116:1, 2, 8, 9 (Amplified Bible)

[465] Psalm 117:1-2 (Amplified Bible)
[466] Psalm 115:1 (Amplified Bible)
[467] Saint Francis de Sales

132

Reading: Psalm 118 ☐ ☐

Let Us Pray . . .

Lord Jesus Christ, eternal King, divine and human, crucified for humanity, look upon me with mercy and hear my prayer, for I trust in You. Have mercy on me, for the depth of Your compassion never ends.[468] You, Christ, are the King of Glory, the eternal Son of the Father. You are seated at God's right hand in glory.[469] Make me to know Your ways, O Lord and teach me Your paths.[470]

O God, the King eternal, who divides the day from the night and turns the shadow of death into the morning: Drive far from me all wrong desires, incline my heart to keep Your law, and guide my feet into the way of peace. O God, who is the Author of peace and Lover of order, in whose service is perfect freedom: Defend me, Your humble servant, in all assaults of my enemies, that I, trusting in Your defense, may not fear the power of any adversaries, through the might of Jesus Christ our Lord. Amen.

O give thanks to the Lord, for You are good, for Your mercy and loving-kindness endure forever! Let those now who reverently and worshipfully fear You as their Lord say that Your mercy and loving-kindness endure forever. The Lord is my Strength and Song; and You have become my Salvation. This is the day that You, Lord, have brought about; I will rejoice and be glad in it. Save now, I ask You, O Lord; send now prosperity, O Lord, and give to me success, after Your definition and will![471]

---

[468] Attributed to Saint Ambrose
[469] From *Te Deum Laudamus*
[470] Psalm 25:3

[471] Psalm 118:1,4, 14, 24, 25 (Amplified Bible)

Lord, because You have made me, I owe You the whole of my love; because You have redeemed me, I owe You the whole of myself. Because You have promised so much, I owe You all my being. I pray You, Lord, make me taste by love what I taste by knowledge; let me know by love what I know by understanding. I owe You more than my whole self, but I have no more, and by myself I cannot render the whole of it to You. Draw me to You, Lord, in the fullness of love. I am wholly Yours by creation; make me all Yours, too, in love.[472]

Forgive me my sins, O Lord; forgive me the sins of my youth and the sins of my age, the sins of my soul and the sins of my body, my secret and my whispering sins, my presumptuous and my crying sins, the sins that I have done to please myself, and the sins I have done to please others. Forgive me the sins which I know, and those sins which I know not; forgive them, O Lord, forgive them all of Your great goodness.[473] O Lord, the house of my soul is narrow; enlarge it, that You may enter in. It is ruinous, O repair it! It displeases Your sight; I confess it, I know. But who shall cleanse it, to whom shall I cry but to You? Cleanse me from my secret faults, O Lord, and spare Your servant from strange sins.[474]

O God, from whom to be turned is to fall, to whom to be turned is to rise, and in whom to stand is to abide for ever: grant me in all my duties today Your help, in all my perplexities this day Your guidance, in all my dangers Your protection, and in all my sorrows Your peace; through Jesus Christ our Lord.[475]

---

[472] Anselm, 1033-1109
[473] Lancelot Andrewes, 1555-1626
[474] Augustine, 354-430
[475] Augustine, 354-430

Reading: Psalm 119:1-64 ☐ ☐

Let Us Pray . . .

I lie down in peace and take my rest for it is in You, my God alone, that I dwell unafraid. Your angels guard me through the night and quiet the powers of darkness. Spirit of God be my guide to lead me to peace and glory.

It is but lost labour that I haste to rise up early, and so late take rest, and eat the bread of anxiety. For those beloved of God are given gifts even while they sleep. Glory to You, my God, this night, for all of the blessings of the light. To You, from whom all good does come, my life, my health, my lasting home. Teach me to live, that I may dread the grave as little as my bed. Teach me to die, that so I may rise glorious at the awful day. O may I now on You repose, and may kind sleep my eyelids close; sleep that helps me to vigorously serve my God when I awake. If I lie restless on my bed, Your word of healing peace be said. If powerful dreams rise in the night, transform their darkness into light. All praise to God, sustaining me, redeeming and transfiguring me, Thanksgiving in eternity, all praise, beloved Trinity. Before the ending of the day, Creator of the world I pray that You, with love and lasting light, would guard me through the hours of the night. You have said: Be still and know that I am God, I am the God who heals you in You. O God, I put my trust in you. God You made the earth and heaven, darkness and light. May Your angel guards defend me, slumber sweet Your mercy send me, holy dreams and hopes attend me, this night.

O Lord my God, grant me the grace to desire You with my whole heart, that so desiring, I may seek and find You; and so finding, may love You.[476] Grant, O Lord, that Your love may so fill my

---

[476] Anslem (1109)

life that I may count nothing too small to do for You, nothing too much to give, and nothing too hard to bear, for Jesus Christ's sake.[477]

With my whole heart have I sought You, inquiring for and of You and yearning for You. Oh, let me not ignorantly wander or willfully step aside from Your commandments. I will meditate on Your precepts and have respect to Your paths of life, marked out by Your law. Open my eyes, that I may behold wondrous things out of Your law. My life dissolves and weeps itself away for heaviness. Raise me up and strengthen me according to the promises of Your Word. Give me understanding, that I may keep Your law; yes, I will observe it with my whole heart. Turn away my eyes from beholding vanity, idols and idolatry; and restore me to vigorous life and good health in Your ways. I remember and hold tightly to Your word and the promise to Your servant, in which You have caused me to hope. This is my comfort and consolation in my affliction: that Your word has revived me and given me life. The earth, O Lord, is full of Your mercy and loving-kindness: teach me Your statutes.[478]

God, have mercy on me, a sinner![479] O Lord, forgive what I have been, sanctify what I am, and order what I shall be.[480] O Lord, have mercy upon me, take away my sins, and mercifully kindle in me the fire of Your Holy Spirit. Take away from me the heart of stone, and give me a heart of flesh, a heart to love and adore You, a heart to delight in You, to follow and to enjoy You, for Christ's sake.[481] Lord, grant to the world: Justice, truth and peace.

---

[477] Ignatius Loyola, 1491-1556

[478] Psalm 119:10, 15, 18, 28, 34, 37, 49, 50, 64 (Amplified Bible)

[479] Luke 18.13

[480] Source unknown

[481] Ambrose of Milan, c.339-97

Reading: Psalm 119:65-96 ☐ ☐

Let Us Pray . . .

Oh, may Your love fill and rule my heart. For then there will spring up and be cherished between You and me a likeness of character, and union of will, so that I choose and refuse what You do. May Your will be done in me and me forever.[482]

You have dealt well with Your servant, O Lord, according to Your promise. I pray that Your merciful kindness and steadfast love may be for my comfort, according to Your promise. Let Your tender mercy and loving-kindness come to me that I may live, for Your law is my delight! Forever, O Lord, Your Word is settled in heaven. Your faithfulness is from generation to generation; You have established the earth, and it stands fast.[483]

O merciful God, fill my heart, I pray, with the graces of Your Holy Spirit; with love, joy, peace, patience, gentleness, goodness, faithfulness, humility and self-control. Teach me to love those who hate, to pray for those who despitefully use people, that I might be a child of Your love, my Father, who makes the sun to rise on the evil and the good, and who sends rain on the just and on the unjust. In adversity grant me, and those I love, grace to be patient. In prosperity keep me humble, may I guard the door of my lips today, may I only lightly esteem the pleasures of this world, and mainly thirst after heavenly things; through Jesus Christ my Lord.[484]

O be joyful in the Lord my soul; serve the Lord with gladness and come before

---

[482] Jacobus Merlo, 1597-1664

[483] Psalm 119:65, 76, 77, 89, 90 (Amplified Bible)

[484] Anselm, 1033-1109

His presence with a song. I know that You, Lord, are God, it is You who has made me and not me myself, it is true that I am one of Your chosen people and a sheep of Your pasture. I go on my way through Your gates with thanksgiving and into Your courts with praise. I am thankful to you and seek to speak good of Your name. For You Lord are gracious, Your mercy is everlasting; and Your truth endures from generation to generation.[485]

You are Wisdom, uncreated and eternal, the Supreme First Cause, above all beings, sovereign Godhead, sovereign goodness. Raise me, I pray, that I may totally respond to the supreme, unknown, ultimate, and splendid height of Your Word, mysterious and inspired. There all God's secret matters lie covered and hidden under darkness both profound and brilliant, silent and wise. You make what is ultimate and beyond brightness secretly to shine in all that is most dark. In Your way, ever unseen and intangible, You fill to the full with most beautiful splendor those souls who close their eyes that they may see.[486]

Lord: How do I love You? Let me count the ways. I love You to the depth and breadth and height my soul can reach, when feeling out of sight for the ends of being and of ideal grace. I love You to the level of every day's most quiet need, by sun and candlelight. I love You freely, as people strive for right. I love You purely, as they turn from praise. I love You with a passion put to use in my old griefs, and with my childhood faith. I love You with the breath, smiles, tears, of all my life! And, God, if You choose I shall love You better after death.[487]

O Lord, heavenly Father, in whom is the fullness of light and wisdom, enlighten my mind by Your Holy Spirit, and give me grace to receive Your word with reverence and humility, without which

---

[485] Traditional Jubilate Psalm 100

[486] The Cloud of Unknowing, 14th century (St. Denis's prayer)

[487] Elizabeth Browning, 1806-1861

no person can understand
Your truth, for Christ's
sake.[488]

O Lord, my heavenly Father,
almighty and everlasting
God, who brought me safely
to the beginning of this day:
Defend me with Your mighty
power and grant that this day
I fall into no sin, neither run
into any kind of danger; but
that I, being ordered by Your
governance, may do always
what is righteous in Your
sight, through Jesus Christ
my Lord. Amen.

I go forth into this new day
in the goodness of my
merciful Father, in the
gentleness of my wonderful
Saviour, Jesus, in the radiance
of His Holy Spirit. I set forth
in the wisdom of my all-
seeing Father, in the patience
of my Servant King and
Saviour, and in the truth of
the all-knowing and revealing
Holy Spirit.[489]

---

[488] John Calvin, 1509-64

[489] Adapted from Saint Patrick

Reading: Psalm 119:97-144 ☐ ☐

Let Us Pray . . .

Almighty God, You have given me grace to make my requests to You and You have promised through Your well-beloved Son that if I pray You will hear my prayers: Fulfill now, O Lord, the desires and petitions I present as may be best for me and grant me the knowledge of Your truth.

The grace of the Lord Jesus Christ, and the love of God, and the fellowship of the Holy Spirit, be with all who call upon Your name. May You O God of hope fill me with all joy and peace in believing through the power of the Holy Spirit. Glory to You O God whose power, working in me, can do infinitely more than I could ever ask or imagine: Glory be to You from generation to generation in the Church, and in Christ Jesus forever and ever. Amen.[490]

Holy Spirit, think through me till Your ideas are my ideas.[491] Teach me to do what pleases You, for You are my God, let Your kindly Spirit lead me on a level path.[492]

And now most merciful God, I confess that I have sinned against You in thought, word, and deed, by what I have done, and by what I have left undone. Though I know better, I have not loved You with my whole heart; I have not loved my neighbors as myself. I am truly sorry and I humbly repent. I turn from my wicked ways to instead follow You and your excellent ways. For the sake of Your Son, Jesus Christ, have mercy on me and forgive me; that I might may delight in Your will, and walk in Your ways, to the glory of Your name. Amen. O God make speed to save me.

O my God, give me Your grace so that the things of

---

[490] Romans 15:13; Ephesians 3:20, 21

[491] Amy Carmichael, 1868-1951

[492] Psalm 143:10

this earth and things more naturally pleasing to me, may not be as close as You are to me. Keep my eyes, my ears, my heart from clinging to to things of this world. Break my bonds, raise my heart. Keep my whole being fixed on You. Let me never lose sight of You and while I gaze on You, let my love of You grow more and more every day.[493]

Your word is a lamp to my feet and a light to my path. Accept, I sincerely ask You, the freewill offerings of my mouth, O Lord, and teach me Your ordinances.

Uphold me according to Your promise, that I may live; and let me not be put to shame in my hope! The entrance and unfolding of Your words give light, their unfolding gives understanding, discernment and comprehension to the simple. Establish my steps and direct them by means of Your Word. Let not any iniquity have dominion over me. Make Your face shine with pleasure upon Your servant, and teach me Your statutes. Your righteous testimonies are everlasting and Your decrees are binding to eternity. Give me understanding and I shall live with discernment and comprehension for all of the years given me.[494]

O most merciful redeemer, friend and brother, may I know You more clearly, love You more dearly, and follow You more nearly, for Yours own sake.[495] Grant Lord, that I may not, for one moment, admit willingly into my soul any thought contrary to Your love.[496]

Father, my hope, Son, my refuge, Holy Spirit, my protection, Holy Trinity, glory be to You. Amen.[497]

---

[493] John Henry Newman, 1801-90

[494] Psalm 119:105, 108, 116, 130, 133, 135, 144 (Amplified Bible)

[495] Richard of Chichester, 1197-1253

[496] Edward Bouverie Pusey, 1800-82

[497] Saint Ioanniki

Reading: Psalms 119:145-176 ☐ ☐

Psalm 120 ☐ ☐

Let Us Pray . . .

Jesus, Saviour of the world, come to me in Your mercy. I look to You to save and help me this new day. Come now and dwell with me, Lord Jesus Christ. Hear these prayers, with those prayers offered through the day and be with me in all of my comings and goings.

I have anticipated the dawning of the morning and cried in childlike prayer, I hoped in Your word. Hear my voice according to Your steadfast love. O Lord, give renewed life to me and revive my life in Christ according to Your righteous decrees and the generousity of Your Holy Spirit. Great are Your tender mercies and loving-kindness, O Lord, give me life according to Your ordinances. Let me live that I may praise You, and let Your decrees help me. I have gone astray like a lost sheep, demand of Your servant what You will, for I will not and do not forget Your commandments.[498] Glory to the Father and to the Son, and to the Holy Spirit, as it was in the beginning, is now, and will be forever. Amen.[499]

Lord, give me weak eyes for things which are of no account and clear eyes for all Your truth.[500] From the cowardice that shrinks from new truths, from the laziness that is content with half-truth, from the arrogance that thinks it knows all truth, O God of truth, deliver me today.[501]

O God, You have bound me with others in this bundle of life, give me grace to understand how my life depend on the industry, the honesty and integrity of my fellow-beings that I might be mindful of their needs, grateful for their faithfulness, and faithful in my own

---

[498] Psalm 119:147, 149, 156, 175, 176 (Amplified Bible)

[499] Magnificat Luke 1:46-55

[500] Soren Kierkegaard, 1813-55

[501] Source unknown

responsibilities to them, through Jesus Christ our Lord.[502]

I hear and join in Mary's song, may I be likewise open to Your love and favour: My soul proclaims the greatness of the Lord, my spirit rejoices in You, God my Saviour; for You have looked with favour on Your lowly servant. From this day all generations will call You blessed. The Almighty has done great things for me, and holy is Your name. I serve the same God most high, of whom Mary said: He has mercy on those who fear Him in every generation. He has shown the strength of His arm, He has scattered the proud in their conceit. He has cast down the mighty from their thrones, and has lifted up the lowly. He has filled the hungry with good things, and the rich He has sent away empty. He has come to the help of His servant Israel, for He has remembered His promise of mercy. The promise He made to our fathers, to Abraham and his children forever.

In my distress I cried to the Lord, and He answered me.[503] O heavenly Father, in whom I live and move and have my being: I humbly pray for You to so guide and govern me by Your Holy Spirit, that in all the cares and occupations of my life I do not forget You, but remember that I am ever walking in Your sight; through Jesus Christ my Lord. O God, the author of peace and lover of concord, grant to me to be so firmly established in the love of Yourself, that no trials whatsoever may be able to part me from You.[504] O God, kindle in me the fire of Your love.

---

[502] Reinhold Niebuhr, 1892-1971

[503] Psalm 120:1 (Amplified Bible)

[504] Roman Breviary

Reading: Psalms

121 ☐ ☐   122 ☐ ☐
123 ☐ ☐   124 ☐ ☐
125 ☐ ☐   126 ☐ ☐

Let Us Pray . . .

I will lift up my eyes to the hills --From whence shall my help come? My help comes from the Lord, Who made heaven and earth.[505] I was glad when they said to me, let us go to the house of the Lord![506] So, to You do I lift up my eyes, O You Who isenthroned in heaven.[507] My help is in the name of the Lord, Who made heaven and earth.[508] Do good, O Lord, to those who are good, and to those who are right with You and all people in their hearts.[509] The Lord has done great things for I am glad![510]

All praise to You, my God, this night, for all the blessings of the light! Keep me, O keep me, King of kings, beneath Your own almighty wings. Praise God, from whom all blessings flow. Praise Him, all creatures here below, praise Father, Son, and Holy Ghost.[511] Lord, let me not love in just words and talk; but let my love be true, showing itself in action.[512]

Lord, You have taught me that all my doings without love are worth nothing: Send Your Holy Spirit throughout this night so that tomorrow I might be so filled to overflowing as to pour into hearts this most excellent gift of Your love into the lives of others.

From dullness of conscience, from feeble sense of duty, from thoughtless disregard of consequences to others, from a low idea of the obligations of my calling, and from half-heartedness in my service to You: Save and help me, O LORD. From

---

[505] Psalm 121:1-2 (Amplified Bible)
[506] Psalm 122:1 (Amplified Bible)
[507] Psalm 123:1 (Amplified Bible)
[508] Psalm 124:8 (Amplified Bible)
[509] Psalm 125:4 (Amplified Bible)
[510] Psalm 126:3 (Amplified Bible)

---

[511] Bishop Thomas Ken
[512] 1 John 3.18 (Good News Bible)

self-conceit, vanity, and boasting, from delight in supposed success and superiority, raise me to the modesty and humility of true sense and taste and reality. And from all the harms and hindrances of offensive manners and self-assertion: Save and help me, O LORD.[513]

Lord of grace and gentleness, I pray for a world in which ordinary humanity fails so often. I pray for those who are called government ministers servants in every nation. I pray that those who lead and take on themselves great responsibilities may not simply wish to seem great in the eyes of others, but may genuinely serve their peoples, searching continually for policies and strategies which will be for the good of all, especially for the weakest and most vulnerable. I ask this for the sake of Him who is both servant and Lord, Jesus Christ.[514]

O God, fountain of love, pour Your love into my soul, that may I love those You love with the love You give me, and think and speak with the love You give me, for Jesus Christ's sake.[515]

Christ, Son of the living God, may Your holy angels guard my sleep. May they watch over those I love while we rest and hover over our beds. Reveal to us in our dreams - visions of Your glorious truth, High Prince of the Universe, High Priest of the Mysteries of God. May no dreams disturb our rest, no nightmares darken our dreams. May no fears or worries delay our prompt, willing repose. May the virtue of my daily work honour this evening's prayer. May my sleep be deep and soft so that my work might be fresh and hard in the morrow.[516]

---

[513] From Southwell Litany

[514] Christopher Avon Lamb

[515] Edward Bouverie Pusey, 1800-82

[516] Celtic prayer attributed to Saint Patrick

Reading: Psalms

127 ☐ ☐ 128 ☐ ☐

129 ☐ ☐ 130 ☐ ☐

131 ☐ ☐

Let Us Pray . . .

God of my life, I welcome this new day and You in it. The day is a gift to me, a new creation, a promise of resurrection. I thank You for the sleep that has refreshed me. Thank You for new beginnings, full of promise and opportunity. Let me not waste a minute of this gift. Make me alive to the beauty and adventure of it all. During this day keep me thoughtful, prayerful, and may all that I think, feel, choose, and do be pleasing in Your sight. Lord, bless this day for me and everyone with whom I have to do. Make me a blessing to others.[517]

I will give thanks to You, Lord, with my whole heart; I will tell of all Your marvelous works.[518] Almighty and everlasting God, by whose Spirit the whole body of Your faithful people is governed and sanctified: Receive my supplications and prayers so I may truly serve You, through my Lord and Saviour Jesus Christ. Grant that Your love might be made perfect in my weakness today, that I am renewed in Your image and conformed to the pattern of Your Son, Jesus Christ, today.

I well understand that except that Lord builds the house, they labour in vain who build it; except the Lord keeps the city, the watchperson wakes but in vain.[519] I know that blessed is everyone who fears, reveres, and worships the Lord, who walks in His ways and lives according to His commandments.[520] O Lord help me to be a master of myself that I may be a servant of others.[521]

---

[517] Adapted from Congregation of the Most Holy Redeemer

[518] Psalm 9:1

[519] Psalm 127:1 (Amplified Bible)

[520] Psalm 128:1 (Amplified Bible)

[521] Sir Alexander Henry Paterson, 1884-1947

Grant me to recognize in other people, Lord God, the radiance of Your own face.[522] O God of love, I pray You give me love: Love in our thinking, love in my speaking, love in my doing, and love in the hidden places of my soul. Give me love of my neighbours near and far, love of my friends, old and new, love of those with whom I find it hard to bear. And love of those who find it hard to bear with me, love of those with whom I work, and love of those with whom I take my leisure time. Lord give me love in joy, love in sorrow, love in life and love in death; that so at length I may dwell with You, the One who is Eternal Love.[523]

Lord You are uncompromisingly righteous. You have cut away the thick cords by which the wicked might wish to enslave me.[524] Out of the depths have I cried to You, O Lord. Lord, hear my voice. Let Your ears be attentive to the voice of my supplications. If You, Lord, should keep account of and treat me according to my sins, O Lord, who would stand? I wait for You Lord, I expectantly wait, and in Your Word do I hope.[525] LORD, my heart is not haughty, nor my eyes lofty, neither do I exercise myself in matters too great or in things too wonderful for me. Surely I have calmed and quieted my soul, like a weaned child with his mother, like a weaned child is my soul within me. My confidence in You keeps me from fretting.[526]

Glory to God in the highest, and peace to His people on earth. Lord God, heavenly King, Almighty God and Father, I worship You, I give You thanks, I praise You for Your glory.[527]

---

[522] Pierre Teilhard de Chardin
[523] William Temple, 1881-1944
[524] Psalm 129:4 (Amplified Bible)
[525] Psalm 130:1, 2, 5 (Amplified Bible)
[526] Psalm 131:1-2 (Amplified Bible)
[527] From *Gloria in Excelsis*

Reading: Psalms
132 ☐ ☐   133 ☐ ☐
134 ☐ ☐

Let Us Pray . . .

Blessed are You, O Lord my God, Ruler of the universe! Your Word brings on the dusk of evening, Your wisdom creates both night and day. You determine the cycles of time, arrange the succession of seasons, and establish the stars in their heavenly courses. Lord of the Starry Hosts is Your name. Living and eternal God, rule over me always. Blessed be the Lord, whose Word makes the evening fall.   Amen[528]

Lord, You are my pace-setter, I shall not rush. You make me stop and rest for quiet intervals, You provide me with images of stillness, which restore my serenity. You lead me in the ways of efficiency, through calmness of mind, and Your guidance is peace. Even though I have a great many things to accomplish each day, I will not fret for Your presence is here. Your timelessness, Your all-importance will keep me in balance. You prepare refreshment and renewal in the midst of my activity by anointing my mind with Your oils of tranquility, my cup of joyous energy overflows. Surely harmony and effectiveness shall be the fruits of my hours, for I shall walk in the pace of my Lord, and dwell in Your house for ever.[529]

God my Creator, my Centre, my Friend, I thank You for my good life, for those who are dear to me, for those who have gone on ahead, and for all who have helped and influenced me. I thank You for the measure of freedom I have, and for the extent I have autonomy in my life. And most of all I thank You for the gift of faith that is now in me, for my awareness of You and my hope in You. Keep me, I pray, thankful and hopeful and useful until my life ends. Amen

---

[528] Anglican Church of Canada Book of Alternative Services, 1985

[529] Toki Miyashina (based on Psalm 23)

How good and how pleasant it is for people to dwell together in unity![530]

Sovereign Lord of all persons and nations, I pray for rulers and statespersons who are called to leadership among their fellow citizens. Give them vision to see far into the issues of their time, courage to uphold what they believe to be right, and integrity in their words and motives. And may their service to their people promote the welfare and peace of humankind, through Jesus Christ our Lord.[531] I affectionately and gratefully praise the Lord, as a servant of the Lord, I lift up my hands in holiness and to the sanctuary and bless the Lord! ³The Lord bless You out of Zion, even You Who made heaven and earth.[532]

All-wise and all-seeing God, You look upon all my actions, and see all that I do. Enlighten my understanding that I may clearly see what sins I have committed, and what good I have left undone. Move my heart that I may sincerely repent and make amends.

While the cares and tumults of this life are all around about, guide me in all my undertakings by Your Holy Spirit, that I may abide in Your peace, through Jesus Christ our Lord.[533]

Give my body restful sleep and let the work I have done today be sown for an eternal harvest of righteousness for Your Kingdom sake.[534] Lord Jesus, in Your mercy heal me, in Your love and tenderness remake me. In Your compassion bring grace and forgiveness. May Your love prepare me for the beauty of heaven.[535] May Your Kingdom come to earth as it is in heaven.

---

[530] Psalm 133:1 (Amplified Bible)
[531] Basil Naylor
[532] Psalm 134:1-3 (Amplified Bible)
[533] Swedish Liturgy
[534] From a Roman liturgy
[535] Anslem (1109)

Reading: Psalms

135 ☐ ☐   136 ☐ ☐
137 ☐ ☐

Let Us Pray . . .

O Good Jesus, Word of the Father and brightness of His glory, teach me to do Your will and guide me by Your Spirit. Lord, it is undoubtedly true that if I could see and know myself as I am, I would be truly humble. Therefore, I do fittingly humble myself before You now. Please give grace to Your servant.[536]

O God, You have made all the peoples of the earth of one blood, and sent Your blessed Son to preach peace to those who are far off and to those who are near: Grant that people everywhere may seek after You and find You; bring the nations into Your fold. Pour out Your Spirit upon all flesh; and hasten the coming of Your kingdom; through Your Son, Jesus Christ my Lord. O God and Father of all, whole heavens adore You: Let the whole earth also worship You, all nations obey You, all tongues confess and bless You, and men and women, girls and boys, everywhere love You and serve You in peace, through Jesus Christ my Lord. Amen.

Give me, O Lord I pray, a firm faith, unwavering hope, and perfect love. Pour into my heart the spirit of wisdom and understanding, the spirit of counsel and spiritual strength, the spirit of knowledge and true godliness, and the spirit of Your holy reverence. Light eternal, shine in my heart: Power eternal, deliver me from evil. Wisdom eternal, scatter the darkness of my ignorance. Grant that I may ever seek Your face, with all my heart and soul and strength and, in Your infinite mercy, bring me at last to Your holy presence, where I shall behold Your glory and possess Your promised joys.[537]

---

[536] Adapted from Cloud of Unknowing

[537] Alcuin, 738-804

Your name, O Lord, endures forever, Your fame, O Lord, throughout all ages. For the Lord will judge and vindicate Your people, and You will delay Your judgments. You will manifest Your righteousness and mercy and take into favour Your servants and those who meet Your terms of separation unto Yourself.[538] O how I give thanks to the Lord, for You are good. For Your mercies and loving-kindness endure forever. I give thanks to the God of gods, for Your mercy and loving-kindness endure forever. O give thanks to the Lord of lords, for Your mercy and loving-kindness endure forever. To You Who alone does great wonders, for Your mercy and loving-kindness endure forever; O give thanks to the God of heaven, for Your mercy and loving-kindness endure forever![539]

In the name of Jesus Christ, who was never in a hurry, I pray, O God, that You will slow me down, for I know that I live too fast. With all of eternity before me, make me take time to live - time to get acquainted with You, time to enjoy Your blessings, and time to know others.[540] Lord, I do not know what to ask of You. You alone know what are my true needs for this day. You love me more than I myself know how to love. My heart is open to You; visit, help, and fill me, cast me down and raise me up. I offer myself as a sacrifice to You and put all my trust in You.[541]

May the light of Christ my Lord shine in and out from my heart throughout this day.

---

[538] Psalm 135:13-14 (Amplified Bible)

[539] Psalm 136:1-4, 26 (Amplified Bible)

[540] Peter Marshall

[541] Adapted from Philaret of Moscow

Reading:

Psalms 138 ☐ ☐
139 ☐ ☐ **140** ☐ ☐

Let Us Pray . . .

Blessed are You, God, Almighty Lord, who made the sun to give light to the day and brightened the night with shining stars. You have brought me through this long day and led me to the threshold of night; hear my prayer and the prayers of Your people. Forgive me all the sins I have committed deliberately or in weakness. Receive my evening prayers and pour out upon Your adopted child the riches of Your goodness and mercy.[542]

Almighty God, Father of all mercies, I am Your unworthy servant. I give You humble thanks for all Your goodness and loving kindness to me and to all You have made. I bless You for our creation, preservation, and all the blessings of this life; but above all for Your immeasurable love in the redemption of the world by the Lord Jesus Christ; for the means of grace, and for the hope of glory. And, I pray, that You will give me such an awareness of Your mercies, that with a truly thankful heart I will continue to show forth Your praise. Not only with my lips, but in my very life, by giving my all to Your service, and by walking before You in holiness and righteousness all my days, through Jesus Christ my Lord, to whom, with You and the Holy Spirit, be honour and glory throughout all ages. Amen.

Lord, help me not to despise or oppose what I do not understand.[543] Keep watch, dear Lord, with those who work, or watch, or weep this night, and give Your angels charge over those who sleep. Tend the sick, Lord Christ, give rest to the weary, bless the dying, soothe the suffering, pity the afflicted, shield the joyous, and all for Your love's sake. O God, show Your servants the signs of Your presence. Please

---

[542] Adapted from an Orthodox prayer

[543] William Penn, 1644-1718

provide Your Spirit of love, such that in my companionship with those You place before me, Your abounding grace may increasingly be noticed through my love, through Jesus Christ my Lord.

Lord, You are my God; give ear to the voice of my supplications. O God, the Lord and the Strength of my salvation, You have covered my head in the day of battle. I know and rest in confidence that the Lord will maintain the cause of the afflicted, and will secure justice for the poor and needy.[544]

All the kings of the land will give You credit and praise You, O Lord, for they have heard of the fulfilled promises of Your mouth. Yes, they will sing of the ways of the Lord and joyfully celebrate Your mighty acts, for great is the glory of the Lord. You, O Lord, will superintend that which concerns me. Your mercy and loving-kindness, O Lord, endure forever.[545]

O LORD, you have thoroughly searched me and have known me. You know my down sitting and my uprising; You understand my thoughts afar off. I will confess and praise You for You are fearful and wonderful and I praise you for the awful wonder of my birth! Wonderful are Your works. My inner self knows right well. How precious and weighty also are Your thoughts to me, O God! How vast is the sum of them! Search me through and through, top to bottom, O God, and know my heart! Try me and know my thoughts. And see if there is any wicked or hurtful way in me, and lead me in the way everlasting.[546]

My God, I am heartily sorry for having offended You and

---

[544] Psalm 140:6, 7, 12 (Amplified Bible)

[545] Psalm 138:4, 5, 8 (Amplified Bible)

[546] Psalm 139:1, 2, 14, 17, 23, 24 (Amplified Bible)

I detest all my sins because they offend You, my God, who is Good and who deserves my love. I firmly resolve, with the help of Your grace, to sin no more and to avoid every occasion of sin.

I pause for a few moments of silence in your presence Lord . . . . from out of this silence, teach me to be more alert, humble, expectant, than I have been in the past. May I be ever ready to encounter You in quiet, homely ways, in every appeal to my compassion, every act of unselfish love which shows up and humbles my imperfect love, may I recognize You are still walking through the world. Give me that grace of simplicity that alone can receive Your mystery.[547]

---

[547] Evelyn Underhill, 1875-1941

Reading: Psalms
141 ☐ ☐ 142 ☐ ☐
143 ☐ ☐

Let Us Pray . . .

God our Father, by raising Christ Your Son You conquered the power of death and opened for all humanity the way to eternal life. Let my prayers today raise me up and renew my life by the Spirit. I offer this prayer in worship through Jesus Christ, my Lord.[548]

I adore You, O Christ and I bless You, because by Your holy cross You have redeemed the world. Holy God, holy and strong, holy and immortal, have mercy on me. I glory in Your cross, O Lord, and praise and glorify Your holy resurrection. For by virtue of the cross, joy has come to the whole world.[549]

LORD, I call upon You; attend to me and give ear to my voice when I cry to You. Let my prayer be set forth as incense before You, the lifting up of my hands as the evening sacrifice. But my eyes are toward You, O God the Lord. In You do I trust and take refuge, please preserve my life and do not leave it destitute and barren of works that glorify You.[550]

Lord Jesus Christ, who stretched out Your arms of love on the hard wood of the cross that everyone might come within the reach of Your saving embrace, so clothe me in Your Spirit that I, reaching forth my hands in love, may bring those who do not know You to the knowledge and love of You, for the honour of Your name. Passion of Christ, strengthen me. O good Jesus, hear me, hide me within Your wounds and never let me be separated from You.[551]

---

[548] Adapted from Roman liturgy

[549] From Liturgy of Good Friday

[550] Psalm 141:1, 2, 8 (Amplified Bible)

[551] Anima Christi in 14th Century

God guide me with Your wisdom, God chastise me with Your justice, God help me with Your mercy, God protect me with Your strength, God shield me with Your shade, God fill me with Your grace, for the sake of Your anointed Son.[552] O Father, give me the humility to realize my ignorance, admit my mistakes, recognize my need, welcome advice, and accept rebuke. Help me always to praise rather than to criticize, to sympathize rather than to condemn to encourage rather than to discourage, to build rather than to destroy, and to think of people at their best rather than at their worst. This I ask for Your name's sake.[553]

I cry to You Lord with my voice, with my voice I make supplication. When my spirit gets overwhelmed and life's challenges throw full weight on me, then You know and can show my path forward. I need to cry out to You, O Lord, I will say, You are my refuge, my portion in the land of the living. Bring my life out of prison, that I may confess, praise, and give thanks to Your name.[554]

Hear my prayer, O Lord, give ear to my supplications! In Your faithfulness and in Your righteousness answer me. I remember the days of old. I meditate on all Your doings, I ponder the work of Your hands. I spread out my hands to You, my soul thirsts after You like a thirsty land. Cause me to hear Your loving-kindness in the morning, for on You I lean and in You I trust. Cause me to know the way wherein I should walk, for I lift up my inner self to You. [10]Teach me to do Your will, for You are my God, let Your good Spirit lead me into a level country and into the land of uprightness.[555]

---

[552] Source unknown (Early Scottish)

[553] William Barclay

[554] Psalm 142:1, 3, 5, 7a (Amplified Bible)

[555] Psalm 143:1, 5, 6, 8, 10 (Amplified Bible)

Reading: Psalms
144 ☐ ☐ 145 ☐ ☐
146 ☐ ☐

Let Us Pray . . .

Lord it is night. The night is for stillness. Let me be still in Your Holy presence. It is night after a long day. What has been done has been done. What has not been done has not been done, let it be. The night is dark. Let my fears of the darkness of the world and of my own life rest in You. The night is quiet. Let the quietness of Your peace enfold me, all who are dear to me, and all who have no peace. The night announces the morning. Let me look expectantly to a new day, new joys and new possibilities. In Your name I pray. In darkness and in light, in trouble and in joy, help me Father, to trust Your love, to serve Your purpose, and to praise Your name, through Jesus Christ our Lord. Amen.

Gracious God, You have given me much today, grant me also a thankful spirit. Into Your hands I commend myself and those I love. Be with me still, and when I take my rest renew me for the service of Your Son, Jesus Christ.[556] Dear Lord, I thank You for calling me to share with others Your precious gift of laughter. May I never forget that it is Your gift. As Your children are rebuked in their self-importance and cheered in their sadness, help me to remember that Your foolishness is wiser than humankind's wisdom.[557]

Lord, what are we as human beings that You take notice of us? Or the son of man that You take account of him? My life is like a vapour and a breath, my days are as a shadow that passes away. Happy and blessed are the people who are in such a case; yes, happy are the people whose God is the

---
[556] A New Zealand Prayer Book, 1989
[557] Source unknown ('The Clown's Prayer')

Lord![558] Happy am I because I have the help of the God of Jacob. My hope is in the Lord my God, Who made heaven and earth, the sea, and all that is in them, who keeps truth and is faithful forever, who executes justice for the oppressed, who gives food to the hungry. You, Lord, set free the prisoners.[559]

I believe in You God, the Father almighty, creator of heaven and earth. I believe in You Jesus Christ, His only son, my Lord. Jesus You were conceived by the power of the Holy Spirit and born of the Virgin Mary. You suffered under Pontius Pilate, were crucified, died, and were buried. You descended to the dead. On the third day You rose again. You ascended into heaven, and are seated at the right hand of the Father. You will come again to judge the living and the dead. I believe in You Holy Spirit, in the holy catholic Church, in the communion of saints, in the forgiveness of sins, in the resurrection of the body, and in the life everlasting. Amen.[560]

I will extol You, my God, O King; and I will bless Your name forever and ever, with grateful, affectionate praise. You Lord are gracious and full of compassion, slow to anger and abounding in mercy and loving-kindness. You Lord are good to all, and Your tender mercies are over all Your works and the entirety of things created. All Your works will praise You, O Lord, and Your loved ones will bless You! They will speak of the glory of Your kingdom and talk of Your power, to make known to the sons of men God's mighty deeds and the glorious majesty of His kingdom. Your kingdom is an everlasting kingdom, and Your dominion endures throughout all generations. You uphold all those who are fall and raise up all those who are bowed down.[561]

---

[558] Psalm 144:3, 4, 15 (Amplified Bible)
[559] Psalm 146:5-7 (Amplified Bible)
[560] The Apostles' Creed
[561] Psalm 145:1, 8-14 (Amplified Bible)

Reading: Psalm 147 ☐ ☐

Let Us Pray . . .

I pray to You, O Lord; You hear my voice in the morning, at sunrise I offer my prayers and wait for Your answer.[562] In this hour, fill me, Lord, with Your Spirit of mercy and grace, so that rejoicing throughout the whole day, I take delight in Your praise, through Jesus Christ, my Lord.[563]

Yesterday I was crucified with Christ, today I am glorified with Him. Yesterday I was dead with Christ, today I am sharing in His resurrection. Yesterday I was buried with Him, today I am waking with Him from the sleep of death.[564]

Praise the Lord! For it is good to sing praises to You, my God, for You are gracious and lovely. Praise is becoming and appropriate. You heal the broken-hearted and bind up their wounds. You cure their pains and comfort their sorrows. You determine and count the number of the stars. You call them all by their names. Great are You Lord and of great power. Your understanding is inexhaustible and boundless. Lord You take pleasure in those who reverently and worshipfully fear You, in those who hope in Your mercy and loving-kindness.[565] Almighty God, You are all powerful and other's power is but borrowed from You. I call upon You for all those who hold office that, holding it first as a assignment from You, they may use this appointment or election for the general good and to Yours honour, through Jesus Christ our Lord.[566]

O God, You are the Author and Fountain of Hope, enable me to rely with

---

[562] Psalm 5:2-3

[563] Sarum Breviary

[564] Gregory of Nazianzus (389)

[565] Psalm 147:1-11 (Amplified Bible)

[566] William Tyndale, c.1494-1536 (adapted)

confident expectation on Your promises, knowing that the trials and hindrances of the present time are not worthy to be compared with the glory that shall be revealed, and having my face steadfastly set towards the light that shines more and more to the perfect day, through Jesus Christ our Lord.[567] As has been prayed by others Lord: Give me, Lord, a bit of sun. A bit o' work and a bit of fun. Give me, in the struggle and splutter, my daily bread and a bit of butter. Give me health, my keep to make, and a good bit to spare for poor folks' sake. Give me sense, for I am too often a duffer, and a heart to feel for all that suffers.[568]

Lord my God, give me the will to obey Your commandments, to be faithful to You, and to serve You in the morning with all my heart and soul.[569]

Risen Christ, please give me Your peace. Risen Christ, please be my Peace today.

---

[567] A Devotional Diary

[568] Source unknown

[569] Adapted from Joshua 22

**Reading: Psalms 148 ☐ ☐
149 ☐ ☐ 150 ☐ ☐**

Let Us Pray . . .

Praise the Lord! I sing to You a new song. I praise You in the assembly of Your loved ones! For You take pleasure in Your people. You will beautify the humble with salvation and adorn the wretched with victory. Let me be joyful in the glory and beauty which You confer on me, let me sing for joy upon my bed.[570]

Lord, I believe in You: increase my faith. I trust in You: strengthen my trust. I love You: let me love You more and more. I am sorry for my sins: deepen my sorrow. I worship You as my first beginning, I long for You as my last end. I praise You as my constant helper, and call on You as my loving protector. Guide me by Your wisdom, correct me with Your justice, comfort me with Your mercy, and protect me with Your power.

Lord, I offer You my thoughts to be fixed on You. My words to have You for their theme. My actions to reflect my love for You; my sufferings to be endured for Your greater glory. I want to do what You ask of me, in the way You ask, for as long as You ask, because You ask it. Lord, enlighten my understanding, strengthen my will, purify my heart, and make me holy. Help me to repent of my past sins and to resist temptation in the future. Help me to rise above my human weaknesses and to grow stronger as a Christian. Let me love You, my Lord and my God. And help me to see myself as I really am, a pilgrim in this world, a Christian to respect and love all whose lives I touch, those under my authority, my friends and my enemies. Help me to conquer anger with gentleness, greed by generosity, apathy by fervour. Help me to forget myself and reach out toward others. Make me prudent in

---

[570] Psalm 149:1, 4, 5 (Amplified Bible)

planning, courageous in taking risks. Make me patient in suffering, unassuming in prosperity.

Lord, keep me attentive at prayer, temperate in food and drink, diligent in my work, firm in my good intentions. Let my conscience be clear, my conduct without fault, my speech blameless, and my life - ordered. Put me on guard against my human weaknesses. Let me cherish Your love for me, keep Your law, and come at last to Your salvation. Teach me to realize that this world is passing, that my true future is the happiness of heaven, that life on earth is short, and the life to come eternal.

Praise the Lord! Praise You God in Your sanctuary; praise You in the heavens of Your power! Praise You for Your mighty acts. Praise You according to the abundance of Your greatness! Let everything that has breath and every breath of life praise the Lord! Praise the Lord! Hallelujah![571]

O Lord, you have leased me life, lend me a heart replete with thankfulness.[572] O King, enthroned on high, Comforter and Spirit of Truth, You who are in all places and fill all things, the Treasure of Blessings and the Giver of Life, come and dwell with me, cleanse me from every stain and save my soul, O Gracious One.[573]

Lord, help me to prepare for death with a proper fear of judgment, but a greater trust in Your goodness. Lead me safely through death to the endless joy of heaven. Grant this through Christ Jesus my Lord. Amen.[574] Praise the Lord! Praise the Lord from the heavens, praise You in the heights! Praise You, all Your angels, praise You, all Your hosts! Let them praise and exalt the name of the Lord, for Your name alone is exalted and supreme! Your glory and majesty are above earth and heaven![575]

---

[571] Psalm 150:1, 2, 6 (Amplified Bible)

[572] William Shakespeare, 1564-1616

[573] Orthodox Prayer

[574] This universal prayer is attributed to Pope Clement XI

[575] Psalm 148:1, 2, 13 (Amplified Bible)

The Blessings of God for Others

I am imagining the first Ascension Sunday. And what a couple of months it had been! Despite knowing what would follow, Jesus' determined His "straightway" and uphill return to Jerusalem, the donkey ride, the last supper, the garden prayer, the betrayal kiss, the skirmish-arrest, the shuttle "trials," the mob rants, the brutal treatment, the regrettable denial, the stations, the cross on the hill, the seven words, the agony observed, the split temple veil and darkness, the despair, the thwarted assignment of guards, the extraordinary early morning report of the risen Christ, the appearances to several, and later sightings by many, in Jerusalem, on the road, and in Galilee by the water. Then what would later be seen as His departing words – the Commandment reiterated, and the Commission clarified – in Bethany district. All this yo-yo-ing activity in just a few weeks and days would make your head spin if you were one of the remaining disciples . . . then in a fashion contrasting the unobserved but unquestionably real, physical, and historical resurrection, Jesus was taken up into heaven before their very eyes. As He spoke of power that would come with the Holy Spirit – He lifted His hands and blessed them; and as He blessed[576] them, He left them, scripture says.[577]

These events, culminating in His blessing and ascension

---

[576] Origins of word "bless" meant "on bended knee"

[577] Luke 24:50-52

evoked wonderment, worship, joy, and praise in His followers. The profound event was punctuated with the appearance of two beings who questioned their staring at the sky, understandably awaiting to see what might happen next! We don't have a record of the precise words of the benediction[578] that He pronounced but we do read that Jesus lifted up His hands and blessed them. He did so in His going to sit on the right hand of the Majesty on high, where He continues to bless and make intercession for us, as our Advocate, Redeemer, and Coming King. When I get e-mails from Christian friends, the closing word(s) before their name is often "blessings" or "bless you." In many instances it is a good-bye (formerly *God-bye* or *God be with you*). A request for Divine favour is something I am always pleased to receive (an understatement, of course).

There are curses and there are blessings. We have the God ordained gift of being able to bless others in His name, whether present with us or at a distance. The blessings in this section can be prayed with particular people or with persons in mind. Let us pray blessings on others as a habit of our hearts and with the leading of our God who hears and delights in these blessings.

"Bless you" (and its variations) is such a common expression, appearing over 500 times in Holy Scriptures. There is a particularly famous and unique blessing that appears in Numbers 6:22-27. My imagination easily takes me into Jesus' last earth-spoken benediction. What a moment for He and the disciples. This blessing is one of many that Jesus, the Old Testament scripture quoter, may have used on the first Ascension Day. Nowadays, this passage is often used by priests and ministers who

---

[578] Benediction = "Bene" means "well" and "Dicere" means "to speak"

164

customarily raise their hands (to heaven as an expression of their merely being agents of the Triune God) and say: "The LORD bless you and keep you; the LORD make His face to shine upon you, and be gracious to you; the LORD lift up His countenance upon you and give you peace." These are the same words found in 1979 by archeologists working in the Valley of Ainnom, south of Jerusalem – etched into a credit card sized amulet plaque (probably from 7th Century CE/BC). Amazing! Aaron and his sons were entrusted with the privilege of passing along this prayer of truth, encouragement, and grace, from God to the Israelites. They didn't bestow the blessing when they spoke it – they pronounced and carried it, as channels, from God to the beneficiaries. I believe those who love God and are called according to His purposes have the same stewardship and agentic role.

As indicated, there are many blessings in scripture and in use amongst communities of God's people – the Church. I've listed some of these, following these jottings. I further believe each blessing, with message and promise, should be regularly released by God's people to certain and all people, for His Kingdom sake. As indicated, we can curse or we can bless: The service of blessing others is such a great gift from the Giver of Gifts. The royal priesthood of believers are accorded the responsibility to bless others as a means for their flourishing, transformation and well-being. This invites the benefits and blessings of God the Father, God the Son, and God. the Holy Spirit into the lives of others.

May grace and eternal life be with all those who love our Lord Jesus Christ.[579]

May the God of peace cause you to thrive, to mature, and become holy; and may you be kept safe and blameless in spirit, soul and body, for the coming of our Lord Jesus Christ. God has called you and He will not fail you.[580]

May our Lord Jesus Christ and God our Father, who loved us and in His grace gave us unfailing courage and a firm hope, encourage you and strengthen you to always do and say what is good.[581]

May the Lord Himself, who is our source of peace, give you peace at all times and in every way. The Lord be with you all.[582]

Now the God of peace, who brought again from the dead our Lord Jesus Christ, that Great Shepherd of the sheep, through the blood of the everlasting covenant, make you mature and cause you to flourish in every good work to do His will, working in you that which is well-pleasing in His sight; to whom be glory for ever and ever.[583]

The God of all grace, who has called you to His eternal glory in Christ . . . support, strengthen and establish you. To Him be the power for ever and ever.[584]

May God the Father and Jesus Christ, the Father's Son,

---

[579] Ephesians 6.24 (Jerusalem Bible)

[580] 1 Thessalonians 5.23-4 (Jerusalem Bible)

[581] 2 Thessalonians 2.16-17 (Good News Bible)

[582] 2 Thessalonians 3.16 (Good News Bible)

[583] Hebrews 13.20-21 (Authorized Version)

[584] 1 Peter 5.10-11 (New Revised Standard Version)

give us grace, mercy, and peace; may these be yours in truth and love.[585]

Peace be with you.[586] God bless you.[587]

Grace be to you and peace, from Him who is, who was, and who is to come, from the seven spirits before His throne, and from Jesus Christ, the faithful witness, the first-born from the dead.[588]

Go in peace: the wisdom of the Wonderful Counsellor guide you, the strength of the Mighty God defend you, the love of the Everlasting Father enfold you, the peace of the Prince of Peace be upon you. And the blessing of God Almighty, Father, Son, and Holy Spirit be upon you all this night and for evermore.[589]

May the road rise to meet you, may the wind be always at your back, may the sun shine warm upon your face, may the rains fall softly upon your fields. Until we meet again, may God hold you in the hollow of His hand.[590]

Our Lord Jesus Christ be near You to defend You, within You to refresh You, around You to preserve You, before You to guide You, behind You to justify You, above You to bless You, who lives and reigns with the Father and the Holy Ghost, God for evermore.[591]

God be your comfort, your strength; God be your hope

---

[585] 2 John 3 (Good News Bible)
[586] 3 John 15
[587] James 2.16 (Good News Bible)
[588] Revelation 1.4-5 (Revised English Bible)
[589] Source unknown
[590] Source unknown (Celtic)
[591] Source unknown

and support; God be your light and your way. And the blessing of God, Creator, Redeemer and Giver of life, remain with you now and for ever.[592]

May God the Father bless you; may Christ take care of you; the Holy Spirit enlighten you all the days of your life. The Lord be your Defender and Keeper of body and soul, both now and for ever, to the ages of ages.[593]

The peace of God, which passes all understanding, keep your heart and mind in the knowledge and love of God, and of His Son Jesus Christ our Lord: and the blessing of God Almighty, the Father, the Son, and the Holy Ghost, be with you and remain with you always.[594]

The grace of our Lord Jesus Christ, and the love of God, and the fellowship of the Holy Ghost, be with you all evermore.[595]

Go forth into the world in peace; be of good courage; hold fast that which is good; render to no person evil for evil; strengthen the fainthearted; support the weak; help the afflicted; honour all persons; love and serve the Lord, rejoicing in the power of the Holy Spirit. And the blessing of God Almighty, the Father, the Son, and the Holy Ghost, be upon you, and remain with you for ever.[596]

May the cross of the Son of God, which is mightier than all the hosts of Satan and more glorious than all the hosts of heaven, abide with

---

[592] Anglican Church in Aotearoa, New Zealand and Polynesia. A New Zealand Prayer Book

[593] The Book of Cerne, 10th century

[594] Church of England. Book of Common Prayer

[595] Church of England. Book of Common Prayer (based on 2 Corinthians 13.13)

[596] Church of England. Book of Common Prayer (with the Additions and Deviations Proposed in 1928)

you in your going out and your coming in. By day and night, at morning and at evening, at all times and in all places may it protect and defend you: From the wrath of evildoers, from the assaults of evil spirits, from foes visible and invisible, from the snares of the devil, from all passions that beguile the soul and body: may it guard, protect and deliver you.[597]

May the grace of the Lord Jesus sanctify you and keep you from all evil; may He drive far from you all hurtful things, and purify both your soul and body; may He bind you to Himself by the bond of love, and may His peace abound in your heart.[598]

May the infinite and glorious Trinity, the Father, the Son, and the Holy Spirit, direct your good works, and after your journey through this world, grant you eternal rest with the saints.[599]

The Lord bless you, and preserve you from all evil, and bring you to everlasting life; and may the souls of the faithful, through the mercy of God, rest in peace.[600]

Go, and know that the Lord goes with you: let Him lead you each day into the quiet place of your heart, where He will speak with you; know that He loves you and watches over you that He listens to you in gentle understanding, that He is with you always, wherever you are and however you may feel: and the blessing of God- Father, Son and Holy Spirit – be yours forever.[601]

---

[597] Church of India, Pakistan, Burma and Ceylon. Book of Common Prayer
[598] Gregorian Sacramentary, 6th century
[599] Mozarabic Liturgy, 7th century
[600] Sarum Primer
[601] Still Waters, Deep Waters

May the love of the Lord Jesus draw you to Himself; may the power of the Lord Jesus strengthen you in His service; may the joy of the Lord Jesus fill your soul; and may the blessing of God Almighty, the Father, the Son and the Holy Ghost, be with you and abide with you always.[602]

Oh, the depth of the riches of the wisdom and knowledge of God! How unsearchable His judgments, and His paths beyond tracing out! Who has known the mind of the Lord? Or who has been His counsellor? Who has ever given to God, that God should repay Him? For from Him and through Him and to Him are all things. To Him be the glory for ever![603]

To the King eternal, immortal, invisible, the only God, be honour and glory for ever and ever.[604]

To Him who is the blessed and only potentate, the King of kings and Lord of lords; who only has immortality, dwelling in the light which no person can approach; whom no person has seen, nor can see: be honour and power everlasting.[605]

Now unto Him who is able to keep you from falling, and to present you faultless before the presence of His glory with exceeding joy, to the only wise God our Saviour, be glory and majesty, dominion and power, both now and ever.[606]

O God, make the door of this house wide enough to receive all who need human love and friendship, but narrow enough to shut out all

---

[602] William Temple, 1881-1944

[603] Romans 11:33-36 (New International Version)

[604] 1 Timothy 1.17 (Revised English Bible)

[605] 1 Timothy 6.15-16 (Authorized Version, adapted)

[606] Jude 24-25 (Authorized Version)

envy, pride, and malice. Make its threshold smooth enough to be no stumbling-block to children, nor to straying feet, but strong enough to turn away the power of evil. God, make the door of this house a gateway to Your eternal kingdom. Grant this through Christ my Lord.[607]

Peace to this house from God our heavenly Father. Peace to this house from His Son who is your peace. Peace to this house from the Holy Spirit the Life-giver. And the peace of the Lord be always with you.[608]

May the wonderful energy of God's healing power flow into you, fill you with new life, and give you peace and calm.[609]

May the healing power of our risen Lord, Jesus Christ, fill your whole being, body, mind and spirit. May He take away all that hurts or harms you, and give you His peace.[610]

May the grace of the Lord Jesus sanctify you and keep you from all evil; may He drive far from you and those you love all hurtful things, and purify both your soul and body; may He bind you to Himself by the bond of love, and may His peace abound in your heart.[611]

May the light of Christ, rising in glory, scatter the darkness of your heart and mind; and may the blessing of God, the Father, the Son and the Holy Spirit, rest upon you, and be with you always.[612]

---

[607] Thomas Ken (1637-1711)

[608] Traditional

[609] Source unknown

[610] Source unknown

[611] *Gregorian Sacramentary*, 6th century

May the risen Lord Jesus watch over you and renew you as He renews the whole of creation. May your heart and life echo His love.[613]

May Christ dwell in your heart through faith; and may you be rooted and grounded in love, and comprehend, with the saints, what is the breadth and length and height and depth of the love of Christ, so that you may be filled with all the fullness of God.[614]

The love of the Lord Jesus draw you to Himself, the power of the Lord Jesus strengthen you in His service, the joy of the Lord Jesus fill your heart; and the blessing of God almighty, the Father, the Son, and the Holy Spirit, be with you and remain with you always.[615]

May the road rise up to meet you, may the wind be always at your back, may the sun shine upon your face, the rains fall soft upon your fields and, until we meet again, may God hold you in the palm of His hand.[616]

The peace of God which passes all understanding, keep your heart and mind in the knowledge and love of Jesus Christ our Lord; and the blessing of God Almighty, the Father, the Son and the Holy Spirit, be upon you and remain with you always.[617]

The Lord bless you and keep you, The Lord make His face to shine upon .you and be gracious to you. The Lord lift up the light of His countenance upon you and give you peace, now and always.[618]

---

[612] Ancient Western Rite for Easter

[613] Celebrating Common Prayer

[614] Based on Ephesians 3:17-19

[615] The Alternative Service Book 1980: By William Temple (1881-1944)

---

[616] Ancient Irish Blessing

[617] Based on Philippians 4:7

[618] Numbers 6:24-6

As we bless others, we are reminded that it is the person of **Jesus Christ** who **is the Benefit and Blessing.** This is so well expressed in these selected lines from the hymn, *Himself.*[619]

Once it was the blessing, **now it is the Lord;** *once it was the feeling,* **now it is His Word.** *Once His gifts I wanted,* **now the Giver own;** *once I sought for healing,* **now Himself alone.** *Once 'twas painful trying,* **now 'tis perfect trust;** *once 'twas busy planning,* **now 'tis trust prayer;** *once for self I laboured,* **now for Him alone.** *Once I hoped in Jesus,* **now I know He's mine;** *once my lamps were dying,* **now they brightly shine.** *Once for death I waited,* **now His coming hail;** *and my hopes are anchored, safe within the vail.*

---

[619] A.B. Simpson, "Himself" In *Hymns of the Christian Life*, p. 248

Concerns Petitions, Supplications and Intercessions

For Creation

- Harvest
- Natural resources
- Environmental concerns
- Natural disasters
- Seasonal weather
- Restoration of planet
- Consumption
- Renewal of resources
- The sky, land, and waters
- Stewardship of all created things

For the World

- Places and people at war
- Circumstances of injustice
- Experiences of hunger
- Experiences of disease
- Circumstances of racial strife
- World governments
- International crises
- International relief organizations
- International organizations
- Senior and elder statespersons
- Peace-makers

Sustainable Development Goals

- Eradication of extreme poverty and hunger
- Achievement of universal primary education
- Promotion of gender equality and empowerment of women
- Reduction of child mortality
- Improved maternal health
- Combatting of HIV/AIDS, malaria and other diseases
- Ensuring environmental sustainability
- Development of global partnerships for development

For the Nation

- Courts and judges
- National leaders
- Elections
- Military personnel
- Advocates for justice and peace
- Leaders of the public service
- National business and social sector leaders

- Indigenous leaders and peoples
- Circumstances of injustice and poverty
- Circumstances of hunger and homelessness
- New and establishing immigrants

For the Province/State/Local Community

- Provincial/State leaders
- Justice leaders, workers & the whole justice sector
- Social services leaders, workers & the whole social services sector
- Health care leaders, workers & the whole health care sector
- Education leaders, workers & the whole education sector
- Civil servants
- Business sector, social sector and service organizations
- Local governments and public services
- Reduction of homelessness & poverty: Issues and situations
- Reducton of racial strife
- Schools, hospitals and human services institutions
- Fire, police, ambulance, utilities workers and services

For the Church Universal

- Persecuted Church and persecuted persons
- Christians working in unfriendly places
- Unity of the Church
- Benevolent work
- Work with women and children in difficult circumstances
- Holiness of the Church
- International workers and mission agencies
- Christian education: schools, colleges, universities and seminaries
- Denominations
- Denominational missions & programs
- Christian emergency and relief organizations
- Para-church organizations

For the Local Congregations/Parishes

- Pastor(s), priest(s), deacon(s), and minister(s)
- Bishop(s), superintendent(s), president(s) of denomination(s)
- Boards, councils, synods, committees and governing bodies
- Elders and other lay leaders
- Congregation/Parish staff members
- Teachers
- Caretaker/custodian(s)
- Receptionist(s)
- Stewards of congregation/parish finances
- Musicians, artists and technical support people
- Short term international service participants
- All members and adherents in community witness
- Local outreach and service to community
- Unity of congregation(s)
- New congregations/parishes and those involved
- Ethnic churches
- Churches working with particularly vulnerable people and people groups

For Those with Special Needs

- Those who suffer with physical illness, and those who care for them
- Those who suffer with mental illness, and those who care for them
- Those who are elderly and infirm, and those who care for them
- Those who have suffered abuse, and those who support them
- Those who suffer with addiction, and those who support them
- Those who mourn the death of love one(s), and those who minister to them
- Those who are lonely, and those who care for them
- Those who are homeless, and those who care for them
- Those who are victims of crime, and those who support them
- Those who needs cannot be spoken

- Those who are facing temptations
- Those who live a single persons
- Those who are about to be married or who are newly married
- Those who celebrate their wedding anniversaries
- Those who struggle with marital difficulties
- Those who are divorced or separated
- Those who are widowed
- Those who are separated from spouses and family because of circumstances
- Those whose sexuality is a source of pain
- Those who have felt unloved because of their sexuality or the hateful acts of others
- Those who celebrate the birth of a child
- Those who long for children
- Those who have adopted a child or children
- Those who are adopted
- Those who care for young children
- Those who care for troubled or high risk adolescents
- Those who care for elderly or needy parents
- Those who are just starting school
- Those who are struggling with peer pressure
- Those who are tying to choose an educational or career path
- Those who are leaving home
- Those who are unemployed or underemployed
- Those who work in business and industry
- Those who work in homemaking
- Those who work in health care
- Those who work in education
- Those who work in agriculture
- Those who work in government
- Those who work in service to others
- Those who are beginning a new career

- Those who struggle with their work or their boss(es)
- Those who are seeking new or different work
- Those who are retired or anticipating retirement
- Those who celebrate baptism
- Those who celebrate a renewed faith commitment or profession of faith
- Those who struggle with doubts
- Those who are persecuted for their faith/Faith
- Those who seek spiritual renewal
- Those with family members and friends who do not yet have faith
- Those who travel
- Those who are enjoying leisure and rest
- Those who travel to be present to worship with others
- Those who are new members of faith communities

For Peace and Reconciliation
- For those who are refuges
- For those whose lives have been disrupted by social unrest, violence and corruption
- For those who now suffer the devastation of colonization and discrimination
- For those who seek to be recognized as persons
- For those who are unconscious of their racism and bias towards their fellow humans
- For reconciliation amongst people
- For reparation for wrongs done
- For the grace forgiveness, its giving and receiving
- For peace in families, in communities, within and between nations

Worshipping Jesus Christ

It is just as natural to forget as it is to remember! From time to time it is good to be reminded into whose presence we come when we pray. From time to time, reciting Pastor Lockridge's declaration, as a worshipful prayer, recalling the various names of our Triune God or rehearsing, reflectively, the attributes of God galvanizes my focus on the Lord Jesus Christ's magnificence and infinite worthiness. He is superior, supreme, and so indescribably great; whereas I am small. Yet, He loves me and invites me to meet with Him, to walk and talk with Him along life's way.

You are My King! Do I Really Know You?[620]

I pray: You, my King, were born King. The Bible says You are a Seven Way King. You are the King of the Jews—that's an Ethnic King. You are the King of Israel—that's a National King. You are the King of righteousness. You are the King of the ages. You are the King of Heaven. You are the King of glory. You are the King of kings and You are the Lord of lords. Now that's You, my King.

Well, I wonder if I know You. Do I really know You? I don't want to be mislead.

---

[620] Adapted from S. M. Lockridge (born Shadrach Meshach Lockridge, March 7, 1913 – April 4, 2000) was the Pastor of Calvary Baptist Church, a prominent African American congregation located in San Diego, California, from 1953 to 1993. He is well-known for a six-and-a-half minute description of Jesus Christ, known as "That's my King!" http://www.youtube.com/watch?v=yzqTFNfeDnE

Do I really know You, my King? David said the Heavens declare the glory of God, and the firmament shows Your handiwork. You, my King, are the only one of whom there are no means of measure that can define Your limitless love. No far seeing telescope can bring into visibility the coastline of the shore of Your supplies. No barriers can hinder You from pouring out Your blessing.

You are enduringly strong. Your are entirely sincere. You are eternally steadfast. Your are immortally graceful. Your are imperially powerful. You are impartially merciful. That's You, my King. You are God's Son. You are the sinner's Saviour. You are the centerpiece of civilization. You stand alone in Yourself. You are honest. You are unique. You are unparalleled. You are unprecedented. You are supreme. You are pre-eminent. You are the grandest idea in literature. You are the highest personality in philosophy. You are the supreme problem in higher criticism. You are the fundamental doctrine of historic theology. You are the carnal necessity of spiritual religion. That's You, my King.

You are the miracle of the age. You are the superlative of everything good that I might choose to call You. You are the only one able to supply all my needs simultaneously. You supply strength for the weak. You are available for the tempted and the tried. You sympathize and You save. You are the Almighty God who guides and keeps all His people. You heal the sick. You cleanse the lepers. You forgive sinners. You discharge debtors. You deliver the captives. You defend the feeble. You bless the young. You serve the unfortunate. You regard the aged. You reward the diligent and You beautify the meek. That's You, my King.

Do I really know You? Well, You, my King, are the King of knowledge. You are the wellspring of wisdom. You are the doorway of deliverance. You are the pathway of peace. You are the roadway of righteousness. You are the highway of holiness. You are the gateway of glory. You are the master of the mighty. You are the captain of the conquerors. You are the head of the heroes. You are the leader of the legislatures. You are the overseer of the overcomers. You are the governor of governors. You are the prince of princes. You are the King of kings and You are the Lord of lords. That's You, my King.

Your office is manifold. Your promises are sure. Your life is matchless. Your goodness is limitless. Your mercy is everlasting. Your love never changes. Your Word is enough. Your grace is sufficient. Your reign is righteous. Your yoke is easy and Your burden is light. I wish there were adequate words to describe You . . . but You are indescribable. That's You, my King. You are incomprehensible, You are invincible, and You are irresistible.

I'm come before You to say that the heavens of heavens cannot contain You, let alone some person like me explain You. I can't get You out of my mind. I can't get You off of my hands. I can't outlive You and I can't live without You. The Pharisees couldn't stand You, but they found out they couldn't stop You. Pilate couldn't find any fault in You. The witnesses couldn't get their testimonies to agree about You. Herod couldn't kill You. Death couldn't handle You and the grave couldn't hold You. That's You, my King.

You always have been and You always will be. I'm recalling the fact that You had no predecessor, nor will You have a successor. There's nobody before You and there'll be nobody after You. You can't be impeached and You are not going to resign. That's You, my King! That's You, my King!

Yours is the kingdom and the power and the glory. Well, all the power belongs to You, my King. We are talking about all sorts and manner of power, but in the end all that matters is Your power. Yours is the power. Yes . . . And the glory. I try to get prestige and honour and glory for myself, but the glory is all Yours. Yes! Yours is the Kingdom and the power and glory, forever and ever and ever and ever. How long is that? Forever and ever and ever and ever. . . And when I get through with all of the ever's, then . . . Amen!

Prayer with the Names of God

Let Us Pray: Lord,[621] God Almighty,[622] my Banner,[623] Provider,[624] Healer,[625] and Sanctifier.[626] God,[627] You are LORD (YHWH).[628] God,[629] You the Lord are my Shepherd,[630] my Peace,[631] my Judge,[632] and the Lord my Righteousness.[633] O Godhead,[634] King,[635] You are my LORD God.[636] You are the Lord who is There,[637] the Lord of Hosts,[638] the Mighty One,[639] and the Most High.[640] I love You!

---

[621] Adonai: Master or Lord Gen. 15:2; Ex. 4:10; Judges 6:15; 2 Sam. 7:18-20; Ps. 8, 114:7, 135:5, 141:8, 109:21-28

[622] El Shaddai or God All Sufficient; Gen. 17:1, 2. (Gen. 31:29, 49:24, 25; Prov. 3:27; Micah 2:1; Isa. 60:15, 16, 66:10-13; Ruth 1:20, 21; Rev. 16:7

[623] Jehovah-Nissi: "to glisten," "to lift up," Ex. 17:15; Psalm 4:6.

[624] Jehovah-Jireh: Gen. 22:14

[625] Jehovah-Rophe: Ex. 15:22-26; Jer. 30:17, 3:22; Isa. 61:1

[626] Jehovah-M'Kaddesh: "To make whole, set apart for holiness" Leviticus 20:7-8

[627] Elohim: God as Creator, Preserver, Transcendent, Mighty and Strong: a plural noun, more than two; Gen. 17:7, 6:18, 9:15, 50:24; I Kings 8:23; Jer. 31:33; Isa. 40:1.

[628] Jehovah: The Self-Existent One, "I am Who I am" or 'I will be: Gen. 2:4 Ex.3; Dan. 9:14; Ps. 11:7; Lev. 19:2; Hab. 1:12

[629] El: mighty, strong, prominent: Gen. 7:1, 28:3, 35:11; Nu. 23:22; Josh. 3:10; 2 Sam. 22:31, 32; Neh. 1:5, 9:32; Isa. 9:6; Ezek. 10:5

[630] Psa. 23, 79:13, 95:7, 80:1, 100:3; Gen. 49:24; Isa. 40:11; Jehovah-Rohi: Psa. 23, from "ro'eh" (to pasture).

[631] Jehovah-Shalom: Judges 6:24; Deut. 27:6; Dan. 5:26; I Kings 9:25 8:61; Gen. 15:16; Ex. 21:34, 22:5, 6; Lev. 7:11-21

[632] Psa. 7:8, 96:13; Shaphat: Gen. 18:25

[633] Jehovah-Tsidkenu: Jer. 23:5, 6, 33:16. from "tsidek" which means straight, stiff, balanced - as on scales - full weight, justice, right, righteous, declared innocent.

[634] Theotes: Col. 2:9; Rom. 1:20.

[635] Melekh: Psa. 5:2, 29:10, 44:4, 47:6-8, 48:2, 68:24, 74:12, 95:3, 97:1, 99:4, 146:10; Isa. 5:1, 5, 41:21, 43:15, 44:6; 52:7, 52:10.

[636] Jehovah Elohim: Gen. 2:4; Judges 5:3; Isa. 17:6; Zeph. 2:9; Psa. 59:5

[637] Jehovah-Shammah: Ezek. 48:35.

[638] Jehovah-Sabaoth: The commander of the angelic host and the armies of God. Isa. 1:24; Psa. 46:7, 11; 2 Kings 3:9-12; Jer. 11:20; Rom. 9:29; James 5:4, Rev. 19: 11-16.

[639] Abir: "to be strong" - Gen. 49:24; Deut. 10:17; Psa. 132:2, 5; Isa. 1:24, 49:26, 60:1.

[640] El Elyon: from "to go up" - Deut. 26:19, 32:8; Psa. 18:13; Gen. 14:18; Nu. 24:16; Psa. 78:35, 7:17, 18:13, 97:9, 56:2, 78:56, 18:13; Dan. 7:25, 27; Isa. 14:14.

Jesus[641] Christ,[642] Almighty[643] Saviour,[644] You are the Word of God[645] and the Wisdom of God.[646] You are Wonderful, Counselor, Mighty God, Everlasting Father, Prince of Peace,[647] Ancient of Days,[648] the Angel of the Lord,[649] and the First and the Last.[650] I love You!

Lord,[651] You are the Holy One,[652] You are Jealous,[653] You are my Father.[654] You are the Branch,[655] the God of Seeing,[656] the Righteous One,[657] the Everlasting God,[658] the God of the Covenant,[659] and the Sun of Righteousness.[660] Mighty God,[661] God my Rock,[662] my Stone,[663] my Strength,[664] and my Shield.[665] Lord,[666] God with us,[667] You are the Highest,[668] the Deliverer,[669]

---

[641] Joshua or Y'shua or Je-Hoshua means Jehovah is Salvation

[642] Equivalent to the Hebrew 'Messiah' (Meshiach), The Anointed One

[643] Pantokrator: 2 Cor. 6:18, Revelation 19:6

[644] Soter: Luke 1:4 7

[645] Logos: John l:1; Rev. 19:13

[646] Sophia: Proverbs; I Cor. 1, 2

[647] Isaiah 9:6

[648] 'Attiq Yomin (Aramaic): Dan. 7:9, 13, 22

[649] Theophanies, Christophanies or pre-incarnate appearances of the Son of God Gen. 16:7ff, 21:17, 22:11, 15ff, 18:1-19:1, 24:7, 40, 31:11-13, 32:24-30; Ex. 3:6, 13:21, Ezek. 1:10-13; I Cor. 10:3

[650] Isa. 44:6, 48:12.

[651] Kurios: Found about 600 times in the NT.

[652] Kadosh: "the Holy One of Israel" Psa. 71:22; Isa. 40:25, 43:3, 48:17.

[653] Kanna: zealous; Ex. 20:5, 34:14; Deut. 5:9; Isa. 9:7; Zech. 1:14, 8:2.

[654] 2 Sam. 7:14-15; Psa. 68:5; Isa. 63:16, 64:8; Mal. 1:6.

[655] Tsemach: Zech. 3:8, 6:12; Isa. 4:2; Jer. 23:5, 33:15.

[656] El Roi: The God Who opens our eyes. Gen. 16:13.

[657] Tsaddiq: Psa. 7:9.

[658] El-Olam: God of everlasting time; Gen. 21:33; Psa. 90:1-3, 93:2; Isa. 26:4.

[659] El-Berith: Judges 9:46

[660] Malachi 4:2

[661] El-Gibhor: Isa. 9:6

[662] Tsur: Deut. 32:18; Isa. 30:29

[663] Eben: Gen. 49:24

[664] Eyaluth: Psa. 22:19.

[665] Magen: Psa. 3:3, 18:30.

[666] Despotes: Lu. 2:29; Acts 4:24; 2 Pet. 2:1; Jude 4; Rev. 6:10.

[667] Immanuel or Emmanuel or Imanuel: Isaiah 7:14, 8:8; Matt 1:23.

[668] Hupsistos: Mt. 21:9

[669] Palet: Psa. 18:2.

my Saviour[670] and Redeemer.[671] I love You with my whole heart. Lord, I love You!

O Son of God,[672] Son of Man,[673] Son of David,[674] Lamb of God,[675] You are Author of life,[676] Lion of Judah,[677] King of Kings and Lord of Lords.[678] You are Word of God,[679] Head of the Church,[680] the Prince of Peace,[681] Lion of the tribe of Judah,[682] Angel of His presence,[683] Lord of all,[684] Arm of the Lord,[685] and the Author and Finisher of my faith.[686] I love You!

You are the beginning and end of the creation of God,[687] Bread of life,[688] Lord of glory,[689] Lord of hosts (armies),[690] Lord of the dead and the living,[691] Lord of the Sabbath,[692] Captain of salvation,[693] Captain of the Lord's army,[694] Brightness of the Father's glory,[695] Chosen of God,[696] and the Man of sorrows.[697] Lord I love You! You are the Messenger of the covenant,[698] the Christ of

---

[670] Yeshua: "he will save" - Isa. 43:3.

[671] Gaol: to buy back by paying a price; Job 19:25

[672] Mark 1:1

[673] Matthew 8:20

[674] Matthew 15:22

[675] John 1:29

[676] Acts 3:15

[677] Revelation 5:5

[678] Revelation 17:14; 19:16

[679] Revelation 19:13

[680] Ephesians 5:23

[681] Isaiah 9:6

[682] Revelation 5:5

[683] Isaiah 63:9

[684] Acts 10:36

[685] Isaiah 51:9, 10

[686] Hebrews 12:2

[687] Revelation 3:14; 22:13

[688] John 6:48

[689] James 2:1

[690] Isaiah 44:6

[691] Romans 14:9

[692] Mark 2:28

[693] Hebrews 2:10

[694] Joshua 5:14

[695] Hebrews 1:3

[696] 1 Peter 2:4

[697] Isaiah 53:3

[698] Malachi 3:1

God,[699] Christ, the chosen of God,[700] the Mighty one of Israel,[701] Christ, the power of God,[702] the Mighty to save,[703] Christ, the wisdom of God,[704] Minister of the sanctuary,[705] Christ, the Son of God,[706] Christ, Son of the Blessed,[707] Mighty one of Jacob,[708] Consolation of Israel,[709] Offspring of David,[710] Covenant of the people,[711] Plant of renown,[712] and Power of God.[713] You are the Desire of all nations,[714] Heir of all things,[715] Seed of the woman,[716] God of the whole earth,[717] Head of every human being,[718] Holy one of God,[719] Servant of rulers,[720] Head of the corner,[721] Shepherd and Overseer of souls,[722] and the Holy one of Israel.[723] Lord God, I love You!

Jesus, King of the Jews,[724] Saviour of the body,[725] Saviour of the world,[726] Great Shepherd of the sheep,[727] Head of the body,[728] Seed of David,[729]

---

[699] Luke 9:20

[700] Luke 23:35

[701] Isaiah 30:29

[702] 1Corinthians 1:24

[703] Isaiah 63:1

[704] 1 Corinthians 1:24

[705] Hebrews 8:2

[706] Acts 9:20

[707] Mark 14:61

[708] Isaiah 49:26

[709] Luke 2:25

[710] Revelation 22:16

[711] Isaiah 42:6

[712] Ezekiel 34:29

[713] 1Corinthians 1:24

[714] Haggai 2:7

[715] Hebrews 1:2

[716] Genesis 3:15

[717] Isaiah 54:5

[718] 1 Corinthians 11:3

[719] Mark 1:24

[720] Isaiah 49:7

[721] Matthew 21:42

[722] 1 Peter 2:25

[723] Isaiah 41:14; 54:5

[724] John 19:19; Matthew 27:37

[725] ekklesia, Ephesians 5:23

[726] 1 John 4:14

[727] Hebrews 13:20

[728] Ephesians 1:22, 23; 5:23; Colossians 1:18, 24

[729] 2 Timothy 2:8

Shepherd of Israel,[730] Horn of salvation,[731] Son of the Father,[732] Image of God,[733] Son of the Blessed One,[734] Son of the Highest One,[735] Son of David,[736] Sun of Righteousness,[737] Jesus of Nazareth,[738] Stone of stumbling,[739] Jesus, the Son of God,[740] Jesus, the Son of Joseph,[741] King of Zion,[742] King of Israel,[743] King of Saints,[744] King of kings,[745] and King of glory,[746] I love You!

You are the Wisdom of God,[747] Lamb of God,[748] Word of Life,[749] Light of the world,[750] Light to the Gentiles,[751] Word of God,[752] King of the Jews,[753] Prince of Life,[754] Prince of Peace,[755] Prince of the kings of the earth,[756] and Finisher of faith.[757] You are the First begotten of the dead,[758] Friend of sinners,[759] Rock of Offence,[760] Gift of God,[761] Root of David,[762] Glory of Israel,[763] Root of Jesse,[764]

---

[730] Psalms 80:1
[731] Luke 1:69
[732] 2 John 1:3
[733] Hebrews 1:3
[734] Mark 14:61
[735] Luke 1:32
[736] Matthew 9:27
[737] Malachi 4:2
[738] Mark 1:24; Luke 24:19
[739] 1 Peter 2:8
[740] Hebrews 4:14
[741] John 6:42
[742] Matthew 21:5
[743] John 1:49
[744] Revelation 15:3
[745] 1 Timothy 6:15; Revelation 17:14
[746] Psalms 24:7-10

[747] 1 Corinthians 1:24
[748] John 1:29
[749] 1 John 1:1
[750] John 8:12
[751] Isaiah 42:6
[752] Revelation 19:13
[753] Matthew 2:2
[754] Acts 3:15
[755] Isaiah 9:6
[756] Revelation 1:5
[757] Hebrews 12:2
[758] Revelation 1:5
[759] Matthew 11:19
[760] 1 Peter 2:8
[761] John 4:10
[762] Revelation 5:5; 22:16
[763] Luke 2:32

Rose of Sharon,[765] and the God of Israel, the Saviour.[766] I love You Lord!

You are the Word,[767] Christ,[768] Saviour,[769] Rabbi/Teacher,[770] the Second Adam,[771] Advocate,[772] Lord and Saviour, Jesus Christ,[773] Lord from heaven,[774] Lord Christ,[775] Lord Jesus,[776] Lord Jesus Christ,[777] Lord Jesus Christ our Saviour,[778] Carpenter,[779] and the Carpenter's son.[780] You are the Lord's Christ,[781] Chief Shepherd,[782] the Lord, my redeemer,[783] The Christ (Messiah),[784] the Child,[785] the Man Christ-Jesus,[786] Master,[787] Christ, a King,[788] Christ Jesus,[789] Messiah,[790] Christ Jesus our Lord,[791] Messiah the Prince,[792] and the Nazarene.[793] Only Begotten, the one and only,[794] Emmanuel,[795] God

---

[764] Isaiah 11:10

[765] Song of Songs 2:1

[766] Isaiah 45:15

[767] John 1:1

[768] Matthew 16:16; Matthew 1:16; Luke 9:20

[769] John 4:14

[770] John 1:38, Mark 5:35

[771] 1 Corinthians 15:45

[772] 1 John 2:1

[773] 2 Peter 1:11; 3:18

[774] 1 Corinthians 15:47

[775] Colossians 3:24

[776] Acts 7:59; Colossians 3:17; 1 Thessalonians 4:12

[777] Acts 11:17; 16:31; 20:21; Romans 5:1, 11; 13:14

[778] Titus 1:4

[779] Mark 6:3

[780] Matthew 13:55

[781] Luke 2:26

[782] 1 Peter 5:4

[783] Isaiah 43:14

[784] Matthew 16:20; Mark 14:61

[785] Isaiah 9:6; Luke 2:27, 43

[786] 1 Timothy 2:5

[787] Matthew 23:8

[788] Luke 23:2

[789] Acts 19:4; Romans 3:24; 8:1; 1Corinthians 1:2, 30; Hebrews 3:1; 1Peter 5:10, 14

[790] John 1:41

[791] 1Timothy 1:12; Romans 8:39

[792] Daniel 9:25

[793] Matthew 2:23

[794] John 3:16; John 1:14; John 1:18

[795] Isaiah 7:14, Matthew 1:23

with us,[796] Rabbi, Rabboni,[797] Saviour,[798] and God's dear Son.[799] Oh how I love You! You are the Saviour, Jesus Christ,[800] Jehovah,[801] Jehovah's fellow,[802] Jesus,[803] Jesus Christ,[804] Jesus Christ our Lord,[805] Jesus Christ our Saviour,[806] The Very Christ,[807] Teacher,[808] the Second Man,[809] Holy and Righteous,[810] Mighty God,[811] Almighty,[812] Eternal Father,[813] Wonderful Advisor,[814] and Lord, mighty in battle.[815] You are Lord over all,[816] the Lord, strong and mighty,[817] Lord, our righteousness,[818] Lord, your holy one,[819] Chiefest among ten thousand,[820] Alpha and Omega,[821] Anointed,[822] and Lord.[823] I sing Your praises and tell You that I love You with all of my heart!

You are the Lord our righteousness,[824] Lord God Almighty,[825] the Blessed and

---

[796] Matthew 1:23

[797] John 1:49; 20:16

[798] Luke 2:11

[799] Colossians 1:13

[800] 2 Timothy 1:10; Titus 2:13; 2 Peter 1:1

[801] Isaiah 40:3

[802] Zechariah 13:7

[803] Matthew 1:21

[804] Matthew 1:1; John 1:17; 17:3; Acts 2:38; 4:10; 9:34; 10:36; Romans 1:1, 16:18; 3, 6; 2:16; 5:15, 17; 6:3; 1Corinthians 1:1, 4; 2:2; 2 Corinthians 1:19; 4:6; 13:5; Galatians 2:16; Philippians 1:8; 2:11; 1Timothy 1:15; Hebrews 13:8; 1 John 1:7; 2:1

[805] Romans 1:3; 6:11, 23; 1Corinthians 1:9; 7:25

[806] Titus 3:6

[807] Acts 9:22

[808] John 3:2

[809] 1 Corinthians 15:47

[810] Acts 3:14

[811] Isaiah 9:6

[812] Revelation 1:8

[813] Isaiah 9:6

[814] Isaiah 9:6

[815] Psalms 24:8

[816] Romans 10:12

[817] Psalms 24:8

[818] Jeremiah 23:6

[819] Isaiah 43:15

[820] Song of Songs 5:10

[821] Revelation 1:8

[822] Psalms 2:2

[823] Romans 1:3

[824] Jeremiah 23:6

[825] Revelation 15:3

only Potentate,[826] Apostle,[827] Beloved,[828] Mighty God,[829] Most holy,[830] Most mighty,[831] Christ the Lord,[832] the only Mediator,[833] Counsellor,[834] and only wise God, our Saviour.[835] You are the Overseer,[836] David,[837] Potentate,[838] Deliverer,[839] Physician,[840] Commander,[841] Priest,[842] Prince,[843] Prophet,[844] Forerunner,[845]

Ruler in Israel,[846] God,[847] God blessed forever,[848] God manifest in the flesh,[849] and God my Saviour.[850] You are Governor,[851] Good Master,[852] High priest,[853] Servant,[854] Shepherd,[855] Holy Child,[856] Holy One,[857] Chief Shepherd,[858] Good Shepherd,[859] Great Shepherd,[860] YHWH, I AM THAT I AM,[861] I AM,[862] Israel,[863] King,[864] King over

---

[826] 1 Timothy 6:15
[827] Hebrews 3:1
[828] Ephesians 1:6
[829] Isaiah 9:6
[830] Daniel 9:24
[831] Psalms 45:3
[832] Luke 2:11
[833] 1 Timothy 2:5
[834] Isaiah 9:6
[835] Jude 1:25
[836] 1 Peter 2:25
[837] Jeremiah 30:9
[838] 1 Timothy 6:15
[839] Romans 11:26
[840] Matthew 9:12
[841] Isaiah 55:4
[842] Hebrews 7:17
[843] Acts 5:31
[844] Deuteronomy 18:15, 18; Matthew 21:11; Luke 24:19
[845] Hebrews 6:20

[846] Micah 5:2
[847] John 1:1
[848] Romans 9:5
[849] 1 Timothy 3:16
[850] 1 Timothy 2:3
[851] Matthew 2:6
[852] Matthew 19:16
[853] Hebrews 4:14
[854] Isaiah 42:1
[855] Mark 14:27
[856] Acts 4:30
[857] Psalms 16:10; Acts 3:14
[858] 1 Peter 5:4
[859] John 10:11
[860] Hebrews 13:20
[861] Revelation 1:4
[862] John 8:58
[863] Isaiah 49:3
[864] Matthew 21:5

all the earth,[865] Witness,[866] Lawgiver,[867] Leader,[868] Judge,[869] and You are Eternal Life.[870] Lord I love You!

Your Name is Everlasting Father,[871] Faithful and True,[872] the Faithful Witness,[873] The Faithful and True Witness,[874] Righteous Judge,[875] Righteous Servant,[876] True God,[877] The Truth,[878] The Way,[879] and Wisdom.[880] You are Wonderful,[881] the Word,[882] Elect,[883] Ensign,[884] Firstborn,[885] Ransom,[886] Redeemer,[887] Redemption,[888] Propitiation,[889] Righteousness,[890] First and Last,[891] The Resurrection and the Life,[892] First begotten,[893] and the Just One.[894] I love You! O Salvation,[895] Sanctification,[896] Holy thing,[897] Our Hope,[898] Shiloh,[899] Amen,[900] Angel,[901]

---

[865] Zechariah 14:9

[866] Isaiah 55:4; Revelation 1:5

[867] Isaiah 33:22

[868] Isaiah 55:4

[869] Acts 10:42

[870] 1 John 5:20

[871] Isaiah 9:6

[872] Revelation 19:11

[873] Revelation 1:5

[874] Revelation 3:14

[875] 2 Timothy 4:8

[876] Isaiah 53:11

[877] 1 John 5:20

[878] John 14:6

[879] John 14:6

[880] Proverbs 8:12

[881] Isaiah 9:6

[882] John 1:1

[883] Isaiah 42:1

[884] Isaiah 11:10

[885] Psalms 89:27

[886] 1 Timothy 2:6

[887] Isaiah 59:20

[888] 1 Corinthians 1:30

[889] 1 John 2:2

[890] 1 Corinthians 1:30

[891] Revelation 1:17; 2:8; 22:13

[892] John 11:25

[893] Hebrews 1:6

[894] Matthew 27:19, 24; Acts 3:14; 7:52; 22:14

[895] Luke 2:30

[896] 1 Corinthians 1:30

[897] Luke 1:35

[898] 1 Timothy 1:1

[899] Genesis 49:10

[900] Revelation 3:14

[901] Genesis 48:16; Exodus 23:20, 21

Bright Morning Star,[902] True Light,[903] The Living Bread,[904] Branch,[905] Bridegroom,[906] and the Bright and Morning Star,[907] I worship You. You are the Chief Cornerstone,[908] the Living Stone,[909] Our Passover,[910] the Daysman,[911] the Dayspring,[912] the Day Star,[913] the Morning Star,[914] the Cornerstone,[915] the Precious Cornerstone,[916] the Door,[917] the Foundation,[918] the Fountain,[919] the Rock,[920] the Sanctuary,[921] the Righteous Branch[922] the Star,[923] the Stone,[924] the Guarantee,[925] and the Sure Foundation.[926] You are the Lamb,[927] the True Vine,[928] the Vine,[929] the Unspeakable Gift,[930] the Light, everlasting,[931] Light,[932] the Life,[933] and the Sceptre,[934] I worship You and praise Your holy Name! I love You Lord.

---

[902] Revelation 22:16

[903] John 1:9

[904] John 6:51

[905] Jeremiah 23:5; Zechariah 3:8

[906] Matthew 9:15

[907] Revelation 22:16

[908] 1 Peter 2:6

[909] 1 Peter 2:4

[910] 1 Corinthians 5:7

[911] Job 9:33

[912] Luke 1:78

[913] 2 Peter 1:19

[914] Revelation 22:16

[915] Ephesians 2:20

[916] Isaiah 28:16

[917] John 10:7

[918] Isaiah 28:16

[919] Zechariah 13:1

[920] 1 Corinthians 10:4

[921] Isaiah 8:14

[922] Jeremiah 23:5

[923] Numbers 24:17

[924] Matthew 21:42

[925] Hebrews 7:22

[926] Isaiah 28:16

[927] Revelation 5:6, 8; 7:9, 6:16; 10, 17; 12:11; 13:8, 11; 14:1, 4; 15:3; 17:14; 21:9, 14, 22, 19:7, 9; 23, 27

[928] John 15:1

[929] John 15:1

[930] 2 Corinthians 9:15

[931] Isaiah 60:20

[932] John 8:12

[933] John 14:6

[934] Numbers 24:17